TURNING YOUR WORLD UPSIDE DOWN

Other Books by the Author

Mighty to Save: Discovering God's Grace in the Miracles of Jesus

Encounters with Jesus: When Ordinary People Met the Savior

Faith Victorious: Finding Strength and Hope from Hebrews 11

The Heart of an Executive: Lessons on Leadership from the Life of King David

Turning Back the Darkness: The Biblical Pattern of Reformation

TURNING YOUR WORLD UPSIDE DOWN

KINGDOM PRIORITIES IN THE PARABLES OF JESUS

RICHARD D. PHILLIPS

P.O.BOX 817 • PHILLIPSBURG • NEW JERSEY 08865-0817

Page design by Tobias Design
Typesetting by Michelle Feaster

Printed in the United States of America

Library of Congress Cataloging-in-Publication Data

Phillips, Richard D. (Richard Davis), 1960–
Turning your world upside down : kingdom priorities in the parables of Jesus / Richard D. Phillips.
p. cm.
Includes bibliographical references and index.
ISBN 0-87552-579-2 (pbk.)
1. Jesus Christ—Parables. 2. Christian life—Biblical teaching. 3. Kingdom of God—Biblical teaching. I. Title.

BT375.3 .P48 2003
226.8'06—dc21

2002038436

To

Jonathan Stephen Phillips
Beloved son and brother in Christ

(Luke 9:24)

and to

the One
who opened his mouth in parables,
who uttered hidden things, things from of old

(Ps. 78:2)

Contents

Preface

"These are the people who have turned the world upside down!" That was the complaint against the Christians by those who opposed them in Thessalonica in the time of the apostle Paul, as recorded in Acts 17:6. Would that such a complaint were heard today! The only kind of Christians who make this impact on the world are those who have had their lives turned upside down by Jesus.

That is what Jesus wants to do in the life of everyone who comes to him for salvation—turn it upside down so as to claim it for himself. His call to discipleship is radical and demanding (see Luke 9:23–26), and it entails adopting a whole new set of priorities and attitudes that come from Jesus himself. This kind of language is found all through the New Testament. No committed Christian can deny the claim God makes on the life of everyone who professes faith in Jesus. Paul writes that God intends us "to be conformed to the likeness of his Son" (Rom. 8:29). To this end, one of the chief aims of Scripture is that we should "not conform any longer to the pattern of this world, but be transformed by the renewing of your mind" (Rom. 12:2).

Few portions of Scripture confront our worldly way of thinking while presenting Christ's priorities and attitudes quite so strikingly as the parables of Jesus. Here our Lord challenges our approach to people and to money, to security and success. The parables confront our worldliness with the searching perspective of heaven. Meanwhile, the parables provide rich and helpful instruction in the nature of salvation and the government of Christ's kingdom. They present to us the way of salvation through faith in Jesus, and they show us what kind of lives we must live if we are to follow him in this life. Furthermore, just as they did to Jesus' original audience, the parables search our hearts and try our attitudes, showing us the truth about ourselves as well as pointing the way that God now wants us to go. In this respect, the parables are hard, demanding reflection on our lives and prayerful repentance. But they promise rich blessing to those who sit at Jesus' feet, learn of him, and humbly seek God's grace to do his will.

This is the third of my studies in the Gospels, mainly in Luke, published by P&R Publishing. The first two centered on Jesus' miracles and his encounters with people. I am grateful to add these studies on Jesus' parables. In all of these studies I have sought to place writer and reader at the feet of our Lord Jesus, there to look to him in faith, to know him, and to learn to do his will. May God bless these studies to all who read them, that you may be blessed by him and become a blessing to others in his name.

These messages were first preached in the evening services of Tenth Presbyterian Church in Philadelphia, in the fall months of 2001. I thank the session and congregation for their prayers, love, and encouragement that enable me to devote so much of my labor to the ministry of God's Word. I especially thank the dear brothers with whom I shared the ministry at Tenth, as well as my assistant, Patricia Russell, whose invaluable support greatly helped in the production of this book.

This book is dedicated to my second son, Jonathan Stephen Phillips, now aged two, with prayers that he might come in faith to Jesus and follow him in the way of eternal life. I am grateful to his mother and my bride for so much love and faithful support, as well as to his brother and sister for unceasing joy. I am again indebted to my friends Bruce Bell and Jen Bottoms for their invaluable help in reading and critiquing these chapters. Finally, I give thanks to my Lord Jesus Christ, who not only teaches what we need to know but also fully accomplished the work of our salvation. May he graciously send the Holy Spirit to rearrange our hearts and turn our lives upside down to the glory of his name.

1

A Farmer Sowing Seed

Luke 8:1–18

His disciples asked him what this parable meant. He said, "The knowledge of the secrets of the kingdom of God has been given to you, but to others I speak in parables, so that, 'though seeing, they may not see; though hearing, they may not understand.'" (Luke 8:9–10)

The most difficult and dangerous assignment the prophet Nathan ever received is recorded in 2 Samuel 12. Chapter 11 recounts King David's horrific slide into sin, first with adultery with lovely Bathsheba and then with the murder of her husband, Uriah the Hittite. David had used his vast power to cover up his sin. But it all was seen by God, who sent Nathan to confront the king.

Reproving kings was the sort of thing prophets were called upon to do in the Old Testament. On the whole, however, such interventions were not very effective. Elijah's confrontations with wicked King Ahab led to his exile (1 Kings 17). Isaiah's meeting with faithless Ahaz failed to gain his trust in the Lord (Isa. 7). When Jeremiah's scroll of warning reached the hands of King Jehoiakim, that despot carved it up piece by piece and cast it into the fire (Jer. 36). Nathan, of course, lived long before those prophets, and the strategy he employed might have provided a useful model to the others. Instead of directly accusing David, Nathan approached his subject by means of a parable. He spoke to the king about a rich man who had many sheep, but when a traveler came by he took his poor neighbor's only little lamb to make a meal for the visitor (2 Sam. 12:1–4). Nathan's wisdom in using a parable reveals itself in David's response (2 Sam. 12:5–6):

> David burned with anger against the man and said to Nathan, "As surely as the LORD lives, the man who did this deserves to die! He must pay for that lamb four times over, because he did such a thing and had no pity."

A parable is a true-to-life story designed to make a motivating impression. Parables are effective at getting around our defenses and bringing us to a conclusion that turns our thinking upside down. Nathan's parable caused King David to condemn the thing he himself had done. Only when the parable had achieved this turnaround did the prophet press home his point. Stepping forward he cried, "You are the man!" The result was David's repentance and restoration to God, which is the kind of turnaround Jesus' parables seek to work in the hearts and minds of his hearers.

Parables are a powerful means of teaching and persuading, and so it is no wonder that our Lord Jesus made extensive use of parables. In the Synoptic Gospels—that is, Matthew, Mark, and Luke—the bulk of Jesus' teaching appears in this form. Indeed, Matthew tells us Jesus habitually taught this way, citing Psalm 78:2: "Jesus spoke all these things to the crowd in parables; he did not say anything to them without using a parable. So was fulfilled what was spoken through the prophet: 'I will open my mouth in parables, I will utter things hidden since the creation of the world' " (Matt. 13:34–35).

All through the Gospels we find Jesus teaching in colorful, figurative terms. For this reason it is not always easy to decide what qualifies as a parable and what does not. For the purposes of our studies here from the Gospel of Luke, we will focus mainly on those passages that most formally belong in the category of parable, those in which our Lord tells dramatic stories with a spiritual intent.

Why Parables?

The passage we will first consider contains what is sometimes called the master parable, because in it Jesus tells how we should think about parables as a whole. This comes across in Jesus' answer to the disciples' question in Luke 8:9, to which he replied by making a broad statement about his use of parables:

> His disciples asked him what this parable meant. He said, "The knowledge of the secrets of the kingdom of God has been given to you, but to others I speak in parables, so that,

> " 'though seeing, they may not see;
> though hearing, they may not understand.' "
> (Luke 8:9–10)

You will often hear it said that Jesus used parables to give easy illustrations so the simple people could understand. On this basis, we hear that preachers should tell stories instead of providing the doctrinal teaching we find in the preaching and letters of the apostles. But is that why Jesus taught in parables, to make his message accessible to everyone? "I speak in parables," he said, "so that, 'though seeing, they may not see; though hearing, they may not understand.' " Whether we like it or not—and I assure that a great majority of people do not like it—Jesus says the purpose of his parables is not to make his teaching plain but to make it obscure in the eyes of the great mass of people.

This becomes particularly clear in Matthew's version of this parable. There the disciples asked directly, "Why do you speak in parables?" Jesus replied first with regard to the disciples: "The knowledge of the secrets of the kingdom of heaven has been given to you, but not to them." He went on to quote Isaiah 6:9–10:

> This is why I speak to them in parables:
>
> "Though seeing, they do not see;
> though hearing, they do not hear or understand.
>
> In them is fulfilled the prophecy of Isaiah:
>
> " 'You will be ever hearing but never understanding;
> you will be ever seeing but never perceiving.

For this people's heart has become calloused;
they hardly hear with their ears,
and they have closed their eyes.
Otherwise they might see with their eyes,
hear with their ears,
understand with their hearts
and turn, and I would heal them.' "
(Matt. 13:13–15)

The point is that Jesus spoke in parables because of the callous attitude of his audience. We remember that in these public teaching sessions, Jesus generally faced a mixed audience. Many, such as the Pharisees and the scribes, were actively hostile to him. Others were unsympathetic, and others yet came out of mere curiosity. Still others were only vaguely interested and supportive. A minority were followers who had committed to Jesus, of whom some of the women and the group of twelve disciples formed the core group.

In all the versions of this parable, Jesus speaks of the "secret" or, literally, the "mystery" of the kingdom of God. In New Testament usage, a mystery is a truth that is unknown by men and women apart from divine revelation and illumination. That is why the knowledge of it is "given," as Jesus puts it, and not attained. To the disciples this knowledge was given, by grace and not because they had earned it. To the disciples alone Jesus gave his patient explanations of the parables, just as God's people alone today benefit from the Holy Spirit's illuminating work as these parables are read. To his disciples, those who come to Jesus in faith, the parables were and are a powerful means of revelation and persuasion.

But the others in the crowd had not committed to Jesus, and his use of parables obscured the teaching to them.

Jesus did not explain the parables to the crowds, nor did he give them clear and straightforward instruction. Why is this? Because, he said, "Though seeing, they do not see; though hearing, they do not hear or understand." These were people who fulfilled the prophecy of Isaiah 6, people whose hearts were hard to God. As Matthew 13:15 explains, they made their ears dull; they closed their eyes. They were offended by the truths of the gospel, and they willingly turned away, lest they should be moved to faith, lest they should turn to God and be saved by him. Such people rejected God as he was offered as a Savior, so Jesus spoke in such a way as to confound their unbelief. According to the precedent in Isaiah, this was an advance portion of God's judgment on those whose hearts were closed to him. The same thing is true today: unless we are seeking truth, God will not let us find it. What Saint Anselm taught is especially true of the parables, that faith comes before understanding, for it is faith seeking understanding that receives the truth, is blessed, and is saved.

Therefore we will find that the parables serve a dual function. We have already seen in the example of David and Nathan that they are powerful means of provoking faith and repentance. The parables forcefully reveal spiritual truth to Jesus' disciples who receive them in faith. But they also serve to conceal truth from the unwilling and unbelieving. In this sense, it is not merely we who interpret the parables but the parables that interpret us; our response to them reveals the state of our hearts before God. We especially find this in our first parable, the parable of the soils and the seed. This is a parable that provides an example of the very thing it teaches, for, depending on the state of our hearts, it either provokes blessing through repentance and faith or it works judgment through unbelief.

A Farmer Sowing Seed

While scholars categorize the parables in various different ways, one category they all identify is parables of the kingdom. There are many of these, and they are introduced with telling language, such as, "The kingdom of God is like . . ." These parables of the kingdom tell us about God's saving activity in the world. Our first parable is one of these, as evidenced by Luke's introduction: "Jesus traveled about from one town and village to another, proclaiming the good news of the kingdom of God" (Luke 8:1). The parable introduces us to the theme of God's kingdom through an important and lovely word picture: "A farmer went out to sow his seed" (Luke 8:5).

What a dramatic statement of God's work in the world! God is like a farmer going out into his fields, and as he goes he is scattering seeds. What a philosophy of history this provides! The newspapers and history writers tell us that what matters is the rise and fall of great empires, the affairs of corporations and legislatures and armies. But Jesus says that what matters eternally is that God is going through the world like a farmer scattering seed. While we tend to speak of this as "the parable of the soils," focusing as usual on ourselves, Jesus titles it in Matthew 13:18 "the parable of the sower." The main focus is on the wonder of God's kingdom in this world, like a farmer sowing seeds.

What are these seeds? Jesus tells the disciples in Luke 8:11, "The seed is the Word of God." This is how God's kingdom advances in the world: not by the passing of laws, not through the accumulation of money or worldly power or military might, but rather as God sows his Word in the fields of human hearts. Harry A. Ironside writes, "The word of the truth of the gospel is likened to a seed because it is a living thing. It is the means God uses to produce the new birth . . . and so it produces fruit unto life eternal."[1]

This is something the apostle Paul knew. His ministry was not about pressuring the ruling authorities or raising up some kind of political rebellion. He explained in 2 Corinthians 10:4–5, "The weapons we fight with are not the weapons of the world. On the contrary, they have divine power to demolish strongholds. We demolish arguments and every pretension that sets itself up against the knowledge of God, and we take captive every thought to make it obedient to Christ."

This is what matters most in the world, the preaching and sharing and believing of God's Word, his gospel, which, Paul says, "is the power of God for the salvation of everyone who believes" (Rom. 1:16). What a great mistake it is when Christian people and churches focus their labor on things other than God's Word! There are many good and worthy things we might and even must do. But proclaiming God's Word must always be central for us, for that is how God's kingdom extends. This is what we must preach—not our opinions, not our experience, but God's Word, which we have in the Bible. It may not be impressive to the world any more than it was in Jesus' day. But the little seed of God's Word, when rooted in human hearts, bears with it the promise of a great future and God's power for eternal life. In these first few words of his parable, Jesus already has upended many of the attitudes so prevalent among Christians today.

The Soils of Unbelief

This parable tells us about God's kingdom, but it is most famous for what it says about us. It is a parable of the kingdom, but it is also a parable of caution, one that calls us to self-examination and care for our souls.

Jesus says the seed fell on four kinds of soil. The first three all represent hearts that do not ultimately benefit from the hearing of God's Word: "Some fell along the path; it was trampled on, and the birds of the air ate it up. Some fell on rock, and when it came up, the plants withered because they had no moisture. Other seed fell among thorns, which grew up with it and choked the plants" (Luke 8:5–7).

Jesus explained each of these to the disciples. "Those along the path," he began, "are the ones who hear, and then the devil comes and takes away the word from their hearts, so that they may not believe and be saved" (Luke 8:12). These persons hear but do not believe. Since their hearts, like the path, are hard, the Word is not able to penetrate, and the devil takes it away.

All of our hearts are like this apart from God's saving grace. Paul develops his description of humanity in sin in Romans 1. He states that everybody knows about God but suppresses that truth, plunging into spiritual darkness (Rom. 1:18–20). This culminates in a downward spiral: rejection of God leads to sin, and then sin leads us into a further rejection of God (Rom. 1:21–31). This explains all the commotion in this world, a frantic quest to keep God out of our lives while vainly seeking to fill his place with lesser things. If this is true of men and women as they naturally exist in sin, how can any of us ever have God's Word penetrate our hardened hearts? It can happen only if God in his grace comes to break up our hardened ground. Often it takes a painful loss or a great trial to soften our hearts so that his Word may enter and find a place to grow.

Jesus said that the devil is eager to act upon hardened hearts, quickly seizing the seed before faith can grow. J. C.

Ryle describes satanic influences we are all familiar with: "From him come wandering thoughts and roving imaginations, listless minds and dull memories, sleepy eyes and fidgety nerves, weary ears and distracted attention. In all these things Satan has a great hand."[2] Since that is surely true, we ought to prayerfully seek God's help when we gather for worship. Otherwise we will all too often fail to profit from God's Word because of the potent combination of our sinful nature and spiritual attack.

The second kind of hearer is described in Luke 8:6: "Some fell on rock, and when it came up, the plants withered because they had no moisture." Matthew's version is more expansive, saying the seed "sprang up quickly, because the soil was shallow, but when the sun came up, the plants were scorched, and they withered because they had no root" (Matt. 13:5–6). We see in our churches that many respond to the Word quickly and enthusiastically but never put down firm roots. Their appearance of faith is bright but only temporary, because no deep work has taken place in their souls.

James Montgomery Boice recalled a newspaper report of a man arrested for a number of murders. He had grown up in a bad home, dropped out of school, and gotten into various kinds of trouble. After that, the article said, the man became an evangelical Christian. Then he became a Nazi. Then he joined the Ku Klux Klan. He was planning to become a mercenary overseas but ended up as a serial murderer instead.[3] For this kind of person, being a Christian is just one stop in the journey of an unstable life. During his so-called Christian phase he probably looked like many another believer, singing the hymns fervently, taking notes in his Bible. How could you tell him apart from other, true Christians? Temporarily there is no way to tell the difference, but over time it is our response to trials, Jesus says, that tells the tale.

That is Jesus' emphasis in Luke 8:13. Just as the scorching of the sun causes a rootless plant to die, so trials reveal this kind of temporary and ultimately false believer. "They believe for a while, but in the time of testing they fall away." Trials are important for testing and approving our faith. If you want to know if you are a true Christian, if your faith and religious zeal are real and abiding, then you must consider your reaction to trials. If you are unwilling to stand for Christ when you are mocked, if you are not able to obey God's Word even though you seem to lose out, if you respond to bad times by shunning church and blaming God, then you have reason for concern. But if you know a joy that lasts even in sorrows, a light that shines even in darkness, then you may be comforted about the reality of God's work in your heart to bring you to a true and saving faith.

Undoubtedly all three types of faithless hearts can be found in all of our churches, but this second kind of soil, the shallow ground where the seed springs up quickly only to die, is especially prevalent in evangelicalism today. Is this not the inevitable result of a so-called seeker-sensitive model that refuses to make anyone uncomfortable, that seeks to attract people by all the fun in the church? We are gravely warned here by our Lord not to evangelize people merely because it will be fun and uplifting to be in the church or by presenting Christianity as something that works. We must evangelize on the basis of truth, focusing on God's judgment on sin and his grace through a bloody cross, a message that includes God's refining work through trials to separate us from sin. Only the gospel of truth, not one of excitement and fun, will work deeply on the soul to produce a living, persevering faith.

The third kind of soil is described in Luke 8:7: "Other seed fell among thorns, which grew up with it and choked the plants." Jesus explained in Luke 8:14, "The seed that fell among thorns stands for those who hear, but as they go on their way they are choked by life's worries, riches and pleasures, and they do not mature." Here faith is choked to death. If it endures, it is small and weak and almost without any fruit. Why? Because when Christ was taken into the heart, the thorn bushes of the world were not rooted out to provide space for the seed of God's Word to grow.

Jesus gives three examples of worldly weeds that choke this seed. First come life's worries, including things like careers, family concerns, troubles over the economy or the ecology, the retirement account, the weight loss plan, or the pennant race. Second is riches. Here we have the sad example of the rich young man who came to Jesus seeking eternal life. Learning that his riches must give way to Christ, he turned away sad, the Bible says, "because he was a man of great wealth" (Luke 18:23). "How hard it is for the rich to enter the kingdom of God," Jesus observed (Luke 18:24). Third is pleasure, which in our entertainment age is surely the shovel that digs many spiritual graves. All of these things must be brought before God if we are to be saved, even those callings and endeavors that are lawful and good in themselves. A divided heart, a double mind, one that cannot set aside worries or riches or pleasures to follow Christ, will fail to achieve salvation through an enduring faith.

This book is about how Jesus' parables turn our lives upside down. Part of that transforming process is plucking out the weeds of our worldly affections, and especially of our sins, working to root them out completely. The choking process is a gradual one, and it takes place while we hardly notice. Unless we are actively weeding our hearts, unless

God's Word is upending our worldly priorities, we can be sure this spiritual strangling is taking place. This labor, difficult as it is, cannot wait for later. Beware the thought that things can wait, that you can deal with God once you have made your money and had all your fun, for how full of thorns your heart will have become by then, how little room there will be for the seed of God's Word in your life.

The Good and Fruitful Soil

Finally, Jesus spoke of the good soil. There the seed "came up and yielded a crop, a hundred times more than was sown" (Luke 8:8). He elaborated in Luke 8:15, "The seed on good soil stands for those with a noble and good heart, who hear the word, retain it, and by persevering produce a crop." While the preaching of God's Word is essential, Jesus says, having the right kind of heart to receive it is just as important. This fourth soil prompts a number of points.

First, this parable shows that even Jesus had many who did not respond to his message—apparently even the majority did not. We cannot expect anything different and must not think we have failed if our message is refused. But while three bad soils are represented here, Jesus encourages us with the example of the one good soil. If we will proclaim God's Word, some will receive it in a heart God has prepared. These will be saved and will go on to bear abundant spiritual fruit. We may always be confident in proclaiming God's Word, for he says in Isaiah 55:11, "It will not return to me empty, but will accomplish what I desire and achieve the purpose for which I sent it."

Second, this parable shows that the only sure proof of a true and lasting faith is the fruit that it bears. True believers will bear different measures of fruit—in Matthew's and

Mark's version of the parable Jesus says some will bear thirty, some sixty, and some a hundred times what was sown—but in every case, true faith will bear much lasting spiritual fruit. This takes time, for the growth of a seed into a strong and noble tree is a slow process. It requires perseverance, but where there is true faith there will be spiritual fruit, for as Peter reminds us, it is born "not of perishable seed, but of imperishable, through the living and enduring word of God" (1 Peter 1:23).

Luke amplifies this point in the brief parable added in Luke 8:16–18. Jesus said, "No one lights a lamp and hides it in a jar or puts it under a bed. Instead, he puts it on a stand, so that those who come in can see the light. For there is nothing hidden that will not be disclosed, and nothing concealed that will not be known or brought out into the open" (Luke 8:16–17). In bringing all his true people to salvation, God's purpose is to shine a bright light in the world. By the light we shine the character of our hearts will be revealed. Indeed, the punch line of this whole section appears in Luke 8:18. Jesus concluded, "Therefore consider carefully how you listen." That is the point of the parable of the soils. Only the good soil, with its open heart that hears and believes, is transformed and ultimately bears good fruit.

Third, if we are honest we will respond to this parable by admitting that the first and second and third kinds of soil best describe our hearts. I noted earlier that the parables interpret us, they test and judge us, and here we surely find ourselves condemned. What then should we do? We should recognize the truth about ourselves, confess our hardness of heart to God, our shallowness that withers under trial, the many weeds that grow alongside the seed of God's Word in our hearts, asking God for a new heart that only he can give. Ultimately it is only God who can turn our lives upside down, and he delights to give his mighty grace to those who ask and seek.

This kind of repentance and faith is the response Jesus seeks from those who hear his words. Like David, confronted by Nathan's parable after his great sin with Bathsheba, we should reply, "I have sinned against the LORD" (2 Sam. 12:13). It was for this that Jesus proclaimed, "The kingdom of God is near. Repent and believe the good news!" (Mark 1:15). Indeed, as we break up the hard surface of our hearts, as God's Word plows deeply within, as we repent of our worldliness and sin, then our hearts enter into the category depicted by this good and fruitful soil. It is then we find that God has already begun the work of reordering our lives, his kingdom already reigning in the soil of our hearts.

I mentioned the rich young man who turned away from Jesus, our Lord remarking how hard it is for the rich to be saved. Hearing him, the disciples replied with alarm: "Who then can be saved?" All that might have equally been said about all these three kinds of unworthy soils, about the hard heart and the shallow heart and the heart filled with the thorns of cares and riches and pleasure. But Jesus answered them, "With man this is impossible, but with God all things are possible" (Matt. 19:26). That means God can make your heart right; his plow can make fertile soil of you. Since that is true, we should each turn to God, confessing the truth about our hearts and asking him to give us by his grace the open heart that receives his Word and goes on to bear a rich harvest. If you will do that, you will find that God is already working in you, and he will go on to complete the good work he has begun.

The Good Samaritan

Luke 10:25–37

He wanted to justify himself, so he asked Jesus, "And who is my neighbor?" In reply Jesus said: "A man was going down from Jerusalem to Jericho, when he fell into the hands of robbers." (Luke 10:29–30)

The parables of Jesus hold such a powerful place in the annals of human thought that they provide numerous standard phrases to our lexicon. Just about everyone knows what a prodigal son is. You will often hear people complain about wolves in sheep's clothing. And if you stopped people on the street and asked them what is meant by the expression "a good Samaritan," almost all of them would respond with a fair degree of accuracy.

The good Samaritan is one of Jesus' best known parables. As an expression of moral principle it is matched only by the Ten Commandments and the Sermon on the Mount. It has motivated countless acts of mercy, exposing a pitiless world and challenging Christians to consistency between our creed and our conduct.

Who Is My Neighbor?

Jesus told this parable while conversing with an expert in the law, who had spoken out to test our Lord. "Teacher," he asked, "what must I do to inherit eternal life?" (Luke 10:25). Jesus referred him to the Scriptures, saying, "What is written in the Law? How do you read it?" (Luke 10:26). The lawyer answered with two great Old Testament texts that summarize God's law, Deuteronomy 6:5 and Leviticus 19:18: " 'Love the Lord your God with all your heart and with all your soul and with all your strength and with all your mind'; and, 'Love your neighbor as yourself.' " This is what Jesus taught as the sum of the law, so he commended it to this man for his complete obedience. "You have answered correctly," Jesus replied. "Do this and you will live."

The lawyer, however, wanted to justify himself, that is, he wanted to protect himself from the searching scrutiny of these two great commandments. Therefore he retorted, "Who is my neighbor?" With this, he wanted to narrow the definition of a neighbor and thus lower the standard of God's command to love. We know from the writings of the rabbis the generally accepted answer. A neighbor was another Jew, or at least those Jews who were reputable in their religion and manner of life. Others were not neighbors, and one was under no obligation to love or help them. According to this prejudiced standard of love, the lawyer hoped to justify himself before God under the law.

Jesus' answer made an important statement about all human attempts at self-justification by lowering the standard of God's law. Responding with this famous parable, he provided God's definition of a neighbor. The parable begins with a man traveling down from Jerusalem to Jericho. The road between these cities, 17 miles long, is particularly steep. Jerusalem sits at 2,700 feet above sea level, and Jericho is 820 feet below sea level. All through history bandits and cutthroats have preyed on travelers here; up until recent times reports abound of its dangers. Jesus said the man "fell into the hands of robbers. They stripped him of his clothes, beat him and went away, leaving him half-dead" (Luke 10:30).

This sets the stage for three men who come by, through whom Jesus gives his lesson about love for our neighbor. First, there came a priest. He "happened to be going down the same road, and when he saw the man, he passed by on the other side" (Luke 10:31). The priests were the religious elite, descended from Aaron, who performed the sacrifices in the temple. Many of the priests lived in Jericho, and this priest was probably returning home after his tour of service at the temple in Jerusalem.

There were good reasons for a priest to ignore the injured man. First, by touching an unknown, perhaps even dead man, he ran the risk of ceremonial defilement, which would be inconvenient and embarrassing. He may have feared being himself attacked by the robbers. Perhaps he thought there was nothing he could do. Or the man following after could just as well render aid. Or perhaps he had pressing business that demanded an important person like him to keep moving. For whatever reason, this man who of all men ought to have shown pity, this priest who represented God to the people, instead passed by the man in need. No doubt as he hastened by, he thought, "I will pray for the man, and that will be help enough."

Next came a Levite, one of the lower-ranking members of the priestly establishment and administrators of the temple service. It seems that he drew near to look upon the injured man, yet he too "passed by on the other side."

Between the two of them, the priest and the Levite provide what one writer calls "a general condemnation of official Judaism. . . . Official, pious Judaism had two tries to respond and did not."[1] The injured man was not a neighbor to them; since they did not know him, and since he might be a bother or a danger, he was not a fitting object for their mercy. Jesus' statement in the Sermon on the Mount shows the prevalence of this attitude: "You have heard that it was said, 'Love your neighbor and hate your enemy.' But I tell you: Love your enemies and pray for those who persecute you" (Matt. 5:43–44). This shows how common was the idea that enemies and strangers were unworthy of love.

The two religious leaders offer a choice example of religious hypocrisy and externalism. They had just performed a tour of duty at the temple, where emblems of God's grace were set forth, yet they showed not the slightest measure of mercy and compassion to this man so desperately in need. Undoubtedly they thought themselves pure and pious as they passed by on their way, keeping themselves unsoiled by involvement with this stranger, while in fact they were transgressing the heart of God's law. Christians do the same today when they preach or listen to a sermon about God's love, yet go back to their lives without compassion for the dying world outside the church doors.

The Good Samaritan

In the natural progression of this story a godly layman would next appear, a simple Jew who did what the pious leaders would not. But, as he so often did, Jesus shocked his listeners, presenting not a good Jew but a good Samaritan.

Samaritans were descendants of Israelites who had intermarried with foreigners brought in by the Assyrians, mixing their religions together as well. Samaria was just north of Judea, and this proximity only heightened the animosity. The Jews detested the Samaritans. Contact with one of them was considered just as defiling as eating swine flesh. Samaritans were publicly cursed in the synagogues, and prayers were officially offered to God for their damnation. When Jesus sets forth this Samaritan, it was like commending a Palestinian militant to today's Israelite or a Protestant Irishman to an Irish Catholic. Here is what Jesus said:

> But a Samaritan, as he traveled, came where the man was; and when he saw him, he took pity on him. He went to him and bandaged his wounds, pouring on oil and wine. Then he put the man on his own donkey, took him to an inn and took care of him. The next day he took out two silver coins and gave them to the innkeeper. "Look after him," he said, "and when I return, I will reimburse you for any extra expense you may have." (Luke 10:33–35)

The Samaritan first tended the man's wounds, pouring on oil and wine. Oil soothed the skin, and wine was used as an antiseptic. In this he reminds us of the healing grace of God, of whom the prophet Hosea says: "He will heal us . . .

he will bind up our wounds . . . he will revive us . . . he will restore us, that we may live in his presence" (Hos. 6:1–2). Oil and wine were elements of the thank offerings made in the temple, so the priest and the Levite probably had their own store. But it was the Samaritan who gave of his own for the sake of another in need, and thus, as Kenneth E. Bailey writes, "It is the Samaritan who pours out the true offering acceptable to God."[2]

Second, the Samaritan put the injured man on his own mount and took him to an inn to recover. Undoubtedly this required the Samaritan to walk on the difficult and dangerous journey. He was not deterred by racial hatred, nor by hardship, nor even by danger. His compassion was not stemmed by the cost to himself. Finally, when he arrived at the inn he paid for all the man's needs—two denarii was two days' wages and would pay for almost a month's stay at the inn—and made arrangements for his continued involvement in the man's care.

The parable emphasizes the compassion of the Samaritan, and in this way Jesus gave his definition of a neighbor. We must not ask, "Who is my neighbor?" that is, "To whom am I obligated to show love?" Rather, Jesus turns our perspective upside down, demanding that we inquire, "How might I be a neighbor to this person before me?" The love God commands toward our fellow man does not seek categories, does not erect boundaries between types of people—some whom we consider worthy of our love and others not. Rather, Jesus turns the lens back on us and says, "The issue is your willingness to show compassion, to be a neighbor, not whether the other person qualifies for your love." With this in mind, he turned to the lawyer and demanded, "Which of these three do you think was a neighbor to the man who fell into the hands of robbers?" The expert in the law, unwilling even to utter the word *Samaritan*, was nonetheless forced to acknowledge Jesus' meaning: "The one who had mercy on him." Jesus told him, "Go and do likewise" (Luke 10:36–37).

This parable makes a great statement about compassion, telling us that being a neighbor means more than feeling for the person in need. It means doing, as this Samaritan did in the story. The contrast is clear. Whereas the priest and the Levite "passed him by," the Samaritan stopped to help. Whereas the two held back what they had for themselves, the Samaritan gave liberally and sacrificially to the needy person. You see the point. Followers of Christ are not to be passers-by. We are not to walk past the suffering and the sorrow of this world, or its condemnation, without stopping, without endangering our routine and even ourselves, without bending over to help the man or woman in need. As in the parable, stopping may involve the risk of defilement of one kind or another. But Christians are to remember what Christ has done for them, and instead of passing by we are to reach out healing hands, to lift up with merciful arms, to offer our own mount while we walk beside, to pay with the coin in our pocket for the restoration of our neighbor. If we are to embrace the priorities of Christ's kingdom, and if we understand what Christ has done for us, then no longer can we ignore the needs of people around us. Christians remember that we were strangers to God, that "while we were still sinners, Christ died for us" (Rom. 5:8). We, then, must be willing to suffer death, danger, and inconvenience for the sake of others.

Yet how many of us consider that the great wealth God has given us is meant for our excessive luxury, while many go hungry! How many have gifts and skills they never employ for the sake of the poor and needy! How many are quick to put on emblems of Christ, except for his greatest mark in this world, the sacrificing love that bore the cross for us.

Let me make some observations before moving on. The man in the parable was half-dead, having been waylaid in his journey. This was not an able-bodied person choosing for various reasons to live off the labors of others. Neither did the Samaritan pass the man a dollar bill and then move on. This reminds us not to make overly simplistic statements regarding problems like homelessness in our society. Generally speaking, it is not a prudent expression of love to simply give money to those who may be dependent on drugs or alcohol. Being a neighbor is not about making cheap gestures to make ourselves feel better. It means we have to be involved—individually and corporately—if we are to emulate this good Samaritan. Christians are called to sacrificial ministries of mercy but not to foolish gestures that aim mainly to ease our consciences.

I know a Christian living in a major city who was troubled to walk by so many people in need. Realizing that he could not solve all the problems, he set out to get to know the homeless people who frequented his block. He spent time with them, sat and spoke with them. He often bought them food. On cold nights he tenderly draped their bodies with blankets from his closet, many of which were never returned. Jesus does not call us to solve the problems of the world—nor can we—but merely asks, "Who is your neighbor?" And he calls his disciples to show mercy in his name to the needy they encounter in the world.

How Can I Be Saved?

This parable ranks among the greatest expressions of Christian morality, but if we stop there we will fail to grasp the full message conveyed by this passage. In studying the parables, it is important for us to consider the context, the question or problem to which Jesus is responding. With this in mind we should return to the dialogue between Jesus and the expert in the law.

This dialogue consists of two halves that follow the same pattern. In each half, the lawyer asks Jesus a question, and he does so from false motives. Jesus responds with his own question. The lawyer replies, and Jesus refers that answer back as the solution to the lawyer's initial concern. The first sequence occurs in Luke 10:25–28. "Teacher," he asked, "what must I do to inherit eternal life?" Jesus responded by asking him what the law said, and he gave the correct answer of love to God and love to his neighbor. Jesus referred this back as the answer to his initial question. "You have answered correctly. Do this and you will live." Luke 10:29–37 follows this same pattern. Seeking to justify himself, the lawyer retorted, "And who is my neighbor?" Jesus told the parable and then asked the question, "Which of these three do you think was a neighbor?" When the man agreed that it was the Samaritan, Jesus concluded, "Go and do likewise."

What is remarkable is that both halves of this dialogue have the same theme, namely, justification before God. "What must I do to inherit eternal life?" (from the first sequence) is the same as asking, "How can I be saved?" This is the point of the second sequence as well, since the man "wanted to justify himself." Here is the question of all questions, and the one for which we all must find an answer. J. C. Ryle says:

> It is a question which deserves the principal attention of every man, woman, and child on earth. We

> are all sinners—dying sinners, and sinners going to be judged after death. How shall our sins be pardoned? Wherewith shall we come before God? How shall we escape the damnation of hell? Wither shall we flee from the wrath to come? What must we do to be saved? These are inquiries which people of every rank ought to put to themselves, and never to rest till they find an answer.[3]

Both halves of the dialogue approach this issue of salvation from the perspective of human works. Luke 10:25 says, "What must I do?" and in Luke 10:29 the man's question about who is his neighbor has the intent of lowering the law's requirements to what he thinks he will be able to achieve. Karl Barth rightly says:

> The lawyer does not know that only by mercy can he live and inherit eternal life. He does not want to live by mercy. He does not even know what it is. He actually lives by something quite different from mercy, by his own intention and ability to present himself as a righteous man before God.[4]

This dialogue shows us what happens when someone comes to Jesus seeking to be justified by his or her own works. What Jesus does here, he does to everyone seeking to be saved this way. He directs that person to God's law. "What is written in the Law?" he replies. "How do you read it?" Multitudes have perished in their sins because they have *not* read it. They think God's law teaches a standard that is suited to our capabilities, one that is graded according to what we think is reasonable and attainable. Such people are all around us. They say, "I'm basically a good person, so I deserve to go to heaven." Yet, if they would consult God's law, they would find its message to be quite different, its standard set by God's perfection.

"How do you read the Law?" Jesus asks. One answer is found in Matthew 5:48, where Jesus said, "Be perfect, as your heavenly Father is perfect." This is how God's law deals with us. The righteous God has plainly said, "The soul who sins is the one who will die" (Ezek. 18:4, 20). And the Bible tells us, "All have sinned and fall short of the glory of God" (Rom. 3:23). The psalmist therefore laments, "If you, O LORD, kept a record of sins, O Lord, who could stand?" (Ps. 130:3). But the Bible says that he does; the holy Judge keeps exact records of sin. The Book of Revelation shows that all of us, great and small, will come before God as the books are opened. Revelation 20:12 says, "The dead were judged according to what they had done as recorded in the books." People think they have done some small thing commendably and therefore God owes them heaven. But James 2:10 tells us, "Whoever keeps the whole law and yet stumbles at just one point is guilty of breaking all of it." We have all stumbled at far more than just one point of God's law, and for us its message is one of condemnation.

This lawyer began by asking what he could do to gain eternal life, how he could earn God's approval and reward. Luke tells us he was testing Jesus, no doubt hoping to get Jesus into trouble by denying the law. Far from it! Jesus sent him back to the law, as he does all the self-righteous. When the lawyer answered correctly, saying that we need only love God with the whole of our being and our neighbor as ourselves, Jesus pointed him there and said, "Right! Now go ahead, try to do it!"

All you have to do to earn your way to heaven, this says, is to love God completely. Perhaps you think that is an easy thing to do, something attainable for you? Then test yourself, consider your thoughts for just five minutes, let alone for the entirety of your life. You will find that the one single hardest thing for you to do, the demand of God's law that is furthest from your reach, is to love God with all of your heart and mind and soul and strength. But if you could do that, you then would have to add a corresponding love for all other people. I would ask you to catalogue your thoughts about other people, though I am afraid the content would be inappropriate for public disclosure.

The fact is that we have loved not God but ourselves. We have not loved others but have used them for our selfish interest. The problem, we find, is our hearts. There are horrible sins our hands have never gotten around to but that have taken place countless times in our hearts. And our hearts lie open before God, like a book that is open. "Just love!" people say. Yet by that standard above all others we are condemned indeed. "The hearts of men, moreover, are full of evil," wrote the wise man (Eccles. 9:3), so that the command to love is the thing we as sinners are least able to do. No wonder, therefore, that the lawyer tried to lower the standard of love.

This parable gives us a great lesson in the compassion of the good Samaritan. But the lesson we gain from the self-righteous lawyer is more vital yet. It says that if you come to Jesus seeking to be saved by your works, he will say to you what he said to this man: "Do this and live." If you do not, if you do not fulfill the letter and spirit of the law to the fullest degree—and being by nature a sinner you cannot—then you will not receive eternal life, for "the wages of sin is death" (Rom. 6:23).

The apostle Paul had been like this lawyer. He tells us in Philippians 3:4–6 that he once put his confidence in the flesh—in his circumcision, in his standing as a Pharisee, and in his petty claim to legalistic righteousness. Paul, like the priest and the Levite in this parable, once walked down a road for which he is famous. How much like them he was, confident of his righteousness but unwilling to show mercy to a stranger in need. What made Paul's road, the Damascus Road, different is that there he met the risen Lord Jesus Christ, who opened his eyes to the truth. Paul's meeting with Christ changed him, beginning with his view of his own supposed righteousness. In this matter above all others, Jesus turned his life upside down, and Paul's new understanding of justification became a hallmark of his future ministry as an apostle. He writes in Romans 7:14, "We know that the law is spiritual; but I am unspiritual, sold as a slave to sin." Therefore Paul did what the lawyer in our text would not do. He confessed his sin and cast himself on the saving work of Christ alone: "What a wretched man I am! Who will rescue me from this body of death? Thanks be to God—through Jesus Christ our Lord!" (Rom. 7:24–25).

Paul once had trusted in his attainments and works. But he tells us, in Philippians 3:7–9, "Whatever was to my profit I now consider loss for the sake of Christ. What is more, I consider everything a loss compared to the surpassing greatness of knowing Christ Jesus my Lord, for whose sake I have lost all things. I consider them rubbish, that I may gain Christ and be found in him, not having a righteousness of my own that comes from the law, but that which is through faith in Christ—the righteousness that comes from God and is by faith." Paul learned that all his assets, the things he had trusted for eternal life, were liabilities because of the law's judgment on his sin. And what he had thought was nothing, faith in the Savior God had sent, he now saw as the door to forgiveness and eternal life. In that way the man who previously knew only the words of condemnation—"The wages of sin is death"—learned the gospel's word of grace, as he added, "But the gift of God is eternal life in Christ Jesus our Lord" (Rom. 6:23).

If you come to Jesus, like the lawyer in this passage, seeking to be accepted by your works, you will hear the words Jesus said to him: "Do this and live." But to those who seek forgiveness by God's grace on the cross, Jesus says, "Live, and now do this!" As he speaks, he points to the good Samaritan and his merciful acts of kindness. Jesus bestows salvation as a free gift, purchased by his blood and received by simple faith alone, but the salvation he gives includes a new attitude and new ability to love those around us. Charles Spurgeon correctly explains: "What the law demands of us the gospel really produces in us. The law tells us what we ought to be, and it is one object of the gospel to raise us to that condition."[5] Being saved through faith in Christ, we do not escape the mandate of the law or of this great parable. What we escape is condemnation for our sin, while Christ then comes to live in us "so that in him we might become the righteousness of God" (2 Cor. 5:21).

The Greater Samaritan

Before concluding, I should address the relationship of this parable to our Lord Jesus Christ. Throughout church history, many, if not most, interpreters have allegorized this parable to dramatize the work of our salvation. Saint Augustine's version is perhaps most famous, in which the man on the Jericho Road is Adam and the robber is the devil. The priest and Levite are the Mosaic law, which offers no help, while the Samaritan is Christ, who pours the wine of his blood and the oil of his Holy Spirit. Jesus takes us to the inn of the church, where the innkeeper, the apostle Paul, cares for us until he comes back to restore us in the resurrection. That may be a plausible interpretation, but nothing in Jesus' remarks encourages us to take the parable this way. The practice of such speculative allegory should be avoided, as it will often lead us away from the message of the text.

Yet we see why so many have interpreted the parable this way. Surely we must look upon this good Samaritan and think of the One who did far more, who suffered greater scorn than a Samaritan ever did, who rescued us from a far graver condition than that in which this man on the road was found. Our hearts ought surely to melt at this reminder of Christ's great and tender ministry to us.

Imagine what a debt of gratitude this injured man owed the good Samaritan. We can see him searching him out afterwards, wanting to know and express his thanks to the man who saved his life, perhaps offering an eternal debt of loyalty and love. But we have One whose sacrificing mercy was far greater than this, whose ministry saved not our mortal lives but our immortal souls, if we have trusted in Christ.

The Lord Jesus came not merely out from Jerusalem but down from heaven, to seek out those like you who were lost. He found you utterly condemned by the weight of your sin, and he put that burden not on his donkey but on himself. He paid not two denarii but his heart's blood to heal your wounds. Everyone who trusts in him can say, "[He] loved me and gave himself for me" (Gal. 2:20). And having ascended to the Father, he ministers there still, interceding at the right hand of the Majesty on high, sending forth the Spirit with his love. And, yes, he has promised one day to come back, to take you out of the inn of this world, this temporary lodging, and into the heavenly glory where he is crowned and reigns as king.

Realizing this, how can we fail to respond with grateful love for Jesus, how can we keep the priorities and self-serving values we so long have held? The Son of God has suffered death that we might be saved! "Here I am!" he says. "I stand at the door and knock" (Rev. 3:20). Let us, then, open wide the doors of our hearts, that he might come in with saving power, and that we might live in him and through him and for him, that many might be blessed through the rearrangements he brings when he takes his abode in our hearts.

3

A Parable on Prayer

Luke 11:5–13

Ask and it will be given to you; seek and you will find; knock and the door will be opened to you. For everyone who asks receives; he who seeks finds; and to him who knocks, the door will be opened. (Luke 11:9–10)

Church history shows that those who have dared and achieved great things for God were all men and women of fervent prayer. In the biographies of great preachers and reformers, evangelists and missionaries, you will find without exception a great confidence and diligence in prayer. Martin Luther once said that the only way he accomplished so much was by spending so much time in prayer. Mary Queen of Scots, in opposing the Scottish Reformation, commented that she feared nothing on earth so much as the prayers of John Knox. Howard Taylor said of his missionary father that for forty years the sun never rose over China without God finding Hudson Taylor on his knees.

And yet, I do not hesitate to state that the majority of Christians find prayer a difficult struggle. Martyn Lloyd-Jones concurred, giving this explanation:

> There is perhaps no aspect of our Christian life that so frequently raises problems in people's minds as prayer. And it is right that such should be the case, because prayer is, after all, the highest activity of the human soul. . . . The moment you begin to face what really happens in prayer you find inevitably that it is the profoundest activity in which you have ever engaged.[1]

Prayer is something we have to learn, which is why the disciples asked Jesus, "Lord, teach us to pray" (Luke 11:1). Jesus responded by telling them what we should pray, in Luke's version of the Lord's Prayer:

> He said to them, "When you pray, say:
>
> " 'Father,
> hallowed be your name,
> your kingdom come.
> Give us each day our daily bread.
> Forgive us our sins,
>   for we also forgive everyone who sins
>   against us.
> And lead us not into temptation.' "
> (Luke 11:2–4)

In the verses that follow, Jesus teaches the equally important matters of why and how we should pray. Motivation for prayer is for most of us the most crucial issue, and

Jesus aims to instill in us an eagerness and a confidence in prayer.

The Friend at Midnight

The parable in this passage is often called "the friend at midnight." Jesus began by saying:

> Suppose one of you has a friend, and he goes to him at midnight and says, "Friend, lend me three loaves of bread, because a friend of mine on a journey has come to me, and I have nothing to set before him." (Luke 11:5–6)

In the Orient, few values are esteemed more highly than that of hospitality; one is wholly obliged to feed and provide rest to a traveler. Even poor families will roll out as much of a feast as they can muster on such an occasion, in which the family pride is at stake. Here we have a host who does not have food on hand for an unexpected visitor who arrived at night. There were no grocery stores, so Jesus pictures him going to the house of a neighbor to ask for three loaves of bread. Bread was not only the staple of the people's diet in Jesus' day; it was also the fork and spoon they used to eat the other dishes. Without bread the host could not possibly scrape together a suitable meal.

With that introduction, Jesus shifts the focus to the man who is awakened in the night:

> Then the one inside answers, "Don't bother me. The door is already locked, and my children are with me in bed. I can't get up and give you anything." (Luke 10:7)

This brief reply contains a number of excuses to avoid answering the request. First is the late hour, the door being already locked, to which is added the commotion it would cause in the house. This man's family probably shared a single room, as most did then, and if he goes to the door, talks to his neighbor, and prepares the food, he will surely wake the children. Anyone who has ever had fussy little children knows how anguishing it is to have the phone ring just as their eyes are finally shutting. This man, therefore, has plenty of reasons to turn down the request.

Despite this rationale, it seems that Jesus presents this scene rhetorically; it is a situation calculated to produce a reaction of incredulity. We might rephrase his meaning this way: "Can you imagine, someone receiving such a request and giving an excuse like this not to answer the door and help?" Jesus' hearers could not imagine any such thing. Despite the unwelcome circumstances, the request was completely legitimate, even at that hour, because of the vital demands of hospitality. Arland Hultgren observes, "Hospitality was considered a sacred duty throughout the Mediterranean world of antiquity, even when the visitor was a stranger."[2] The honor of the entire village was at stake, so it was unthinkable that the man would refuse such a request, that he would do anything but get up and provide the bread the man had requested. Jesus therefore concludes, "I tell you, though he will not get up and give him the bread because he is his friend, yet because of the man's boldness he will get up and give him as much as he needs" (Luke 11:8). It is not because the man is a friend that he will answer the request but because of the obligation the request placed upon him.

Luke 11:8 contains a notorious translation difficulty involving the word the New International Version (NIV) renders as "boldness." The Greek word, *anaideia*, is not easily carried over into English, and commentators are thus divided about its meaning in this verse. A traditional view is that the word should be taken as "persistence," an option suggested in the marginal notes of the NIV. In this case, the man opens the door because of the persistence of the one making the request. The weakness of this view is that the man in the parable is not depicted as showing persistence. He asks once, so far as we know. Furthermore, there are almost no instances in Greek literature where this word means "persistence." Indeed, the normal usage of this word requires its translation as something like "shamelessness."

That is why the NIV gives the word as "boldness." There is, however, another difficulty. The Greek text does not make clear to which party this word is assigned. It could be, grammatically, that the request would be granted because of the boldness of the one asking, or it could be because of shamelessness, that is, the sense of honor, of the one who was summoned out of bed. There is much debate on this matter, but I think the latter view is the better one.

If we take the word as signifying the boldness of the asker, then Jesus tells the parable to contrast his disciples with the man who asks so boldly. The parable thus functions as something of a rebuke—they are not bold while the man in the story is. But this view requires that God be compared with a sleepy man who is grouchy and unhappy to be bothered, a view of God that Jesus surely did not espouse. That is not the picture Jesus gives us of God. Under this view, the request is granted not because of the graciousness of the giver but because of the bold insistence of the one who asks. Surely Jesus wants to teach boldness in prayer, yet he grounds this confidence not in our importunity but in the readiness of God to answer prayer.

In the second view, which I prefer, the disciples are compared with the man who asks, but God is contrasted to the man who is dragged out of bed. The Greek word *anaideia* refers to the honor of the friend who is summoned. Jesus' point is that if even a reluctant neighbor, bothered and unhappy about being summoned in the middle of the night, is willing to grant the request, how much more will your gracious heavenly Father grant your requests. If the man in the parable agreed because his honor, his shamelessness, was involved, how much more will God respond to the claim upon his honor when we call on him in prayer.

God's honor *is* involved in our prayers because of the promises he has given. The apostle Peter writes, "He has given us his very great and precious promises" (2 Peter 1:4), and not the least are those concerning prayer. We find them scattered all through the Bible, like flowers blooming along our pathway to prayer, the scent of which commends us to this altar of incense. In Psalm 91:15, God says of the man of faith, "He will call upon me, and I will answer him." Zechariah 13:9 says of Christ's flock, "They will call on my name and I will answer them." Ephesians 2:18 promises that through Jesus Christ, "we have access to the Father by one Spirit." Paul says in Philippians 4:6–7 that when we make our requests to God, "the peace of God, which transcends all understanding, will guard your hearts and your minds in Christ Jesus." Peter therefore urges us, "Cast all your anxiety on him because he cares for you" (1 Peter 5:7).

In light of these promises, God's honor is on the line when a Christian prays. This interpretation of the parable is verified by one of the greatest promises about prayer, which occurs just a few verses later as part of Jesus' same discourse: "Everyone who asks receives; he who seeks finds; and to him who knocks, the door will be opened" (Luke 11:10).

So many of us don't pray because we think it makes no difference; we think of it as some dreary spiritual exercise. But how wrong that is; prayer does make a difference. God promises that he will answer our prayers. That does not mean that God comes under our power in prayer or that he suspends his wisdom about what is good for us. But the Bible forthrightly declares that God will give to us as we ask. James 4:2 tells the sad truth about so many of us: "You do not have, because you do not ask God."

Our problem in prayer is not God's unwillingness. God is not like the man who grudgingly gets up to answer the door, though even that man complied because his honor was at stake. God has made great promises to his people regarding prayer, and his glory is bound up in his willingness to give to us as we ask. Therefore, as Hebrews 4:16 says, "Let us then approach the throne of grace with confidence, so that we may receive mercy and find grace to help us in our time of need."

Our Good Father

God's faithfulness to his honor is the first of two reasons given in this passage why we should pray boldly and confidently. The second reason comes in Luke 11:11–13, in which Jesus argues from the lesser to the greater, from the attitude of a human father to that of our Father in heaven:

> Which of you fathers, if your son asks for a fish, will give him a snake instead? Or if he asks for an egg, will give him a scorpion? If you then, though you are evil, know how to give good gifts to your children, how much more will your Father in heaven give the Holy Spirit to those who ask him!

Two points conspire here to encourage us in prayer. The first has to do with God's character. God is good. A. W. Tozer catalogues God's goodness, writing that he is "kind, cordial, benevolent, and full of good will toward men. He is tenderhearted and of quick sympathy, and His unfailing attitude toward all moral beings is open, frank, and friendly. By His nature He is inclined to bestow blessedness and He takes holy pleasure in the happiness of His people."[3] God's goodness is revealed in creation: the rustle of leaves and the song of birds and the splashes of fish resound daily to the praise of his goodness. God's goodness is revealed in history, wherein evil never really prevails and the upright ultimately triumph, as Psalm 37, for instance, declares.

God's goodness is most supremely revealed in the gift of his Son to die for our sins. God gives the best that he has, the dearest to his heart, for the good of others, even we who have offended him in sin! God is good, and that should make all the difference to those who struggle in prayer. As Paul reasons in Romans 8:32, "He who did not spare his own Son, but gave him up for us all—how will he not also, along with him, graciously give us all things?"

God's character encourages us to pray. But Jesus goes further. He adds the truth that believers are children of God. Here is our greatest reason for confidence. God is not only good, but also he has special reason to direct his goodness toward us. Here we have the added incentive of the relationship into which believers have entered with God. God has become our Father, for as the apostle John writes in his Gospel, "To all who received [Jesus], to those who believed in his name, he gave the right to become children of God" (John 1:12). This was one of John's favorite themes. In his first epistle he exulted in this marvelous fact that ought to fill our hearts as well: "How great is the love the

Father has lavished on us, that we should be called children of God! And that is what we are!" (1 John 3:1).

A father is responsible to provide for his children. His relationship with them is knit together with affection and care. This is Jesus' point. When a child asks for a fish, what kind of father would give him a snake? This may refer to an inedible and unclean eel-like creature that often fouled the nets of fishermen in the Sea of Galilee. This would be something useless and awful for a father to give to a hungry child. "Or," he continued, "if he asks for an egg, will he give him a scorpion?" This comparison seems to rest on the fact that a scorpion, when curled up, roughly resembles an egg. Here would be a gift that was dangerous, and not just worthless. What kind of father would do this? Likewise, we should not fear indifference or harm from our heavenly Father in prayer.

Not all human fathers are good, and children of uncaring fathers often have spiritual struggles. But it is natural for fathers to love and care for their children; to do otherwise is contrary even to our sinful human nature. Even in our decadent age, negligent fathers are held in disrepute everywhere. Therefore Jesus argues in Luke 11:13 that if men, "though you are evil," give good gifts to children who ask, how much more will that be true of God, who is supremely good.

Realizing that God is our loving Father is essential to a healthy Christian life, which is why God's fatherhood is greatly stressed by Jesus and the apostles. When teaching the disciples what to pray, in Luke 11:2, the first word Jesus gave them was "Father." In Matthew's longer version of Jesus' teaching on prayer (Matt. 6:5–15), God as Father occurs no fewer than six times. J. I. Packer therefore does not overstate the situation when he writes:

> If you want to judge how well a person understands Christianity, find out how much he makes of the thought of being God's child, and having God as his Father. If this is not the thought that prompts and controls his worship and prayers and his whole outlook on life, it means that he does not understand Christianity very well at all. . . . "Father" is the Christian name for God.[4]

Many of us crave deeper spiritual intimacy with God, and we can be greatly helped by consciously coming to him as children to our Father. A true father's love is one that lasts forever, in all circumstances, surviving all wrongs and disappointments. A father's love thrives on giving, on protecting, on providing. However estranged by sin, however harmed by actions and words, a father will ever say, "He is still my son"; "She is still my daughter." Realizing that these things are true of God will draw you to him. If you are in Christ through faith, God's only begotten Son, then you are just as loved by God as Jesus is. This is what Jesus said to Mary Magdalene outside the open tomb: "I am returning to my Father and your Father, to my God and your God" (John 20:17). By his death and resurrection, Jesus has brought us into his privileged relationship as well-beloved children of the heavenly Father.

If you have never had a true and loving father on earth, you can have one in heaven through the salvation Jesus gives. Jesus is the well-beloved Son, in whom we are made well-beloved children of God. The writer of Hebrews thus depicts our Savior bringing all his own into God's presence: "Here am I," he says, "and the children God has given me" (Heb. 2:13). This is what Jesus foretold of his ascension, shortly after the resurrection: "I am returning to my Father and your Father, to my God and your God" (John 20:17).

What a difference this makes! We are God's children, and he is our Father! The knowledge of God's fatherly love should transform our attitude toward prayer, making us reverent but also confident of blessing. Philip Graham Ryken puts it this way in his book on prayer:

> Jesus teaches us to call God "Father" and to do so with confidence, even if we have never known a father's love. This is because Jesus knows that a father's love is what we have always longed for. He invites us to become God's beloved child. He teaches us to speak to him as our dear Father. That may be difficult at first, but as you learn to pray to God as your Father, you will experience the healing that only a Father's love can bring.[5]

If you put these two reasons together, you see why Jesus invites believers to be confident and bold in prayer. This is what people are looking for today, though often they look in all the wrong places. Especially, so many seek confidence in a ritual or formula. "If you just pray this prayer God will bless you abundantly," we are informed, to which are added testimonials of people who prayed the mantra and received supposed blessings from God. In Matthew's version of Jesus' teaching on prayer, our Lord described this as praying like the pagans, babbling formulas and thus expecting to be heard (Matt. 6:7–8). The problem with pagans is that they do not know God; the problem with so many Christians today is that they hardly know God any better than do the pagans. This is Jesus' point in these parables—we should be confident in prayer not because of what we are doing or how we are doing it, but because of who God is and what he is like. God is faithful to his promises. For the sake of his honor he will answer those who have a right to call on him, namely, those who come through the blood of Jesus Christ. And God is loving as our Father. He is sure to listen, to care, and to do good to us out of his vast resources and power.

Do you struggle in prayer? Do you wonder how your prayer is ever going to be heard? Then remember who God is and what he is like, and ground your confidence there. That, Jesus teaches, is why we should be eager and open in our prayers to God. He is more faithful to us than the best friend we can have in this world—that is what the parable of the friend at midnight teaches—and he is more loving and good than earthly fathers in even their most faithful treatment of their precious children.

Ask, Seek, Knock

Sandwiched between these great reasons why we should pray—God's honor and his fatherly goodness—is a great exhortation to confidence in prayer. Jesus presents it as a command and a promise, a duty and a blessing: "Ask and it will be given to you; seek and you will find; knock and the door will be opened to you. For everyone who asks receives; he who seeks finds; and to him who knocks, the door will be opened" (Luke 11:9–10).

Our prayers should not consist only of requests—in prayer we should worship God and confess to him our sins, thanking him for his many blessings. Nonetheless we should be utterly unabashed, like children to a father, to ask for things we need. Jesus states this with three commands that escalate in intensity, assuring us of success in each: *ask*, *seek, knock*. In Luke 11:10 he adds the word *everyone* to show how certain and universal should be the confidence of all who come to God in his name: "For everyone who asks receives; he who seeks finds; and to him who knocks, the door will be opened."

First, Jesus tells us to "ask" God, "and it will be given to you. . . . For everyone who asks receives." This invites us to make direct requests of God. Christians should regularly pray for themselves and others, asking for God's help and provision and blessing. The story is told that Alexander the Great was approached by a man in need who asked him for money. The conqueror told him to approach his royal treasurer and make his request; whatever he desired would be provided. Shortly afterward, the treasurer showed up aghast, reporting that the man had sought a vast sum of money. Alexander replied, "He has treated me as a king in asking, and so I shall be as a king to him in giving." Likewise, we do well to make requests of our Father as the Almighty God that he is. In so doing we honor him and accept his invitation to ask and thus receive.

Jesus adds, "Seek and you will find. . . . For everyone who seeks finds." William Hendriksen writes, "Seeking is *asking plus acting*. . . . A person must be active in endeavoring to obtain the fulfillment of his needs."[6] We thus should be seeking the things we ask God for. If we pray for spiritual knowledge, we must also diligently read the Bible. If we ask for a loved one's conversion, we must seek it by speaking to him or her about Christ. If we need money, we should ask but then work hard in efforts to earn it. In this way, confidence in prayer leads to boldness in action.

Finally, Jesus says, "Knock and the door will be opened to you. For . . . to him who knocks, the door will be opened." Here Jesus adds the necessity of persistence.

"Knocking is asking plus acting plus persevering. One knocks again and again until the door is opened."[7] That is how we should pray, asking and seeking and knocking, with confidence in the faithfulness and goodness of our Father in heaven.

The Greatest Gift

Let me conclude by making three observations about what Jesus teaches here regarding prayer. The first has to do with the kinds of things he envisions us praying for. Notice that in the parable of the friend at midnight, the man is driven to make his request by his duty as a host. In Luke 11:11–13, the son asks for necessities from his father—a fish and an egg. In neither case is this a matter of something the asker simply wants. Despite his wonderful promises, Christians should not think God is bound to answer frivolous or self-indulgent prayers. I heard it said recently that God has millions of children but not one grandchild—that is, he does not spoil us, but, as Hebrews 12:6 says, "the Lord disciplines those he loves." My daughter recently laid her hands on a Christmas catalogue, circling countless items she simply had to have. My wife responded by throwing the catalogue away and ordering other things that would be better for her. Similarly, God is not a foolishly indulgent parent.

My second observation has to do with legitimate requests that God has left unanswered. I am keenly aware that many believers have prayed boldly, fervently, faithfully, and persistently without receiving what was asked. They are prayers for good and holy things their heart rightly desires. The Bible says, "If we ask anything according to his will, he hears us" (1 John 5:14), yet that has not seemed to happen. How do we deal with prayers God has left long unanswered?

There are several ways of dealing with this problem, beginning by remembering that God is not limited by time. Psalm 37:4 says, "Delight yourself in the LORD and he will give you the desires of your heart." Yet this is in God's timing, and we must wait for him, ever looking forward to a heaven that is more wonderful than any human mind can conceive. Furthermore, we must remember that God acts by a wisdom that is far higher than our own. We do not know what lies even a single step ahead; God responds to our prayers in accordance with his perfect and exhaustive knowledge of all things. We will never know how his secret wisdom has worked in so many ways for our good, to protect us and shape us and bless us.

In his *Confessions*, Augustine tells of how his godly mother prayed that God would thwart his plans to visit decadent Rome. Augustine was at that time unbridled in his passions and apparently far from faith in Christ. While Monica was praying for him all night, young Augustine stole away and set sail, leaving her feeling angry and forsaken by God. How could God not answer such a prayer from a mother's heart? But it was during that trip to Rome that God answered the prayer most dear to her, for there Augustine was converted and saved. God's ways are beyond our evaluation, and we must trust in him while we wait.

Further yet, God's idea of blessing is often quite different from ours. God prioritizes our spiritual blessing over our temporal blessing; he is ever willing to submit us to temporary hardship for our spiritual and eternal good. The way to cooperate with your prayers, then, is to maintain a quiet and contented trust in God. How often we make idols of things we pray for, desiring the gift above the Giver, and thus inhibiting God from granting our request because it would not be good for us. Arthur W. Pink sums up how we ought to think about the difficult matter of unanswered prayer:

> Prayer is a coming to God, telling Him my *need* (or the need of others), committing my way unto the Lord, and then leaving Him to deal with the case as seems Him best. This leaves God to answer the prayer in whatever way He sees fit, and often, His answer may be the very opposite of what would be most acceptable to the flesh.[8]

The final point I want to make deals with Jesus' closing words in this passage on prayer: "If you then, though you are evil, know how to give good gifts to your children, how much more will your Father in heaven give the Holy Spirit to those who ask him!" (Luke 11:13). We should note this emphasis on the Holy Spirit. Surely our Lord was pointing out the best gift God has for us, his holy, life-giving, and loving Spirit. J. C. Ryle correctly says, "The Holy Spirit is beyond doubt the greatest gift which God can bestow upon man. Having this gift, we have all things, life, light, hope and heaven. Having this gift, we have God the Father's boundless love, God the Son's atoning blood, and full communion with all three Persons of the blessed Trinity."[9]

This surely tells us that we should be especially bold in making spiritual requests from God. Christians should pray for the Spirit's power for godliness, for his help against temptation, for his leading in all things, for his help in our prayers. This is the prayer that we ought to make when we come to the church and begin to hear the sermon—"Lord, send to me your Spirit, that I may see and hear." This is the prayer we ought to make concerning our sins—"Lord, empower me by your Spirit for deliverance from sin's power." This is what we should seek for the fullness of our salvation experience, for "righteousness, peace and joy," which Paul says are all "in the Holy Spirit" (Rom. 14:17). Surely, here, when it comes to God's greatest gift and to the highest concerns of his spiritual kingdom, Jesus' words must be true: "Ask and it will be given; seek and you will find."

Therefore, if you cannot call God your Father because you have not trusted Jesus Christ as your Lord and Savior, there is no excuse for you not to be converted and saved and made a child of God right now. If you have not received the Holy Spirit for salvation and faith, it is only because you have not asked, because you have not sought. In this, above all else, you have not only because you ask not.

If you want God to take you as his precious child, to forgive your sins and to live in you by his Holy Spirit, you have only to ask, and it will surely be given. If you will seek a new life and a peace that is with God and from God, you will surely find it. I tell you on the authority of the Lord Jesus Christ, if you will knock on the door to heaven and eternal life, it will be opened to you. "For everyone who asks receives; he who seeks finds; and to him who knocks, the door will be opened." And then, having been saved by grace and through faith, you will find God a better friend than your closest neighbor, more faithful in love than the best human father, and you will be free to pray to him knowing he is eager to listen and ready to bless all those who come to him in Jesus Christ.

The Rich Fool

Luke 12:13–21

Then he said, "This is what I'll do. I will tear down my barns and build bigger ones, and there I will store all my grain and my goods. . . ." But God said to him, "You fool! This very night your life will be demanded from you. Then who will get what you have prepared for yourself?" (Luke 12:18–20)

The apostle Paul warned his disciple Timothy, "The love of money is a root of all kinds of evil." Through greed, he said, many have suffered great spiritual harm. Bible history supports this with numerous examples. In the time of Joshua, Achan's greed led to the defeat of Israel's army at Ai. Despite his prodigious wisdom, King Solomon was ruined by his love of money. Elisha's servant, Gehazi, was afflicted with leprosy. In the New Testament, Ananias and Sapphira lied to the Holy Spirit because of greed and were slain as a result. Alongside sexual lust and sinful pride, the love of money is one of the chief causes of shipwrecked souls. Therefore we should not be surprised that Jesus' parables target our attitude toward money for scrutiny and reevaluation.

A Warning against Greed

The verses that precede this parable provide a prime example of the love of money. A man called out to Jesus while he was teaching, saying, "Teacher, tell my brother to divide the inheritance with me" (Luke 12:13). How incongruous this was! Jesus was instructing them about great spiritual matters, and the man interrupted him to talk about money. Like so many others, this man's sense of need did not penetrate to his soul; he saw in religion only a means for worldly gain.

Jesus refused to comply with this request, citing the limits of his office: "Man, who appointed me a judge or an arbiter between you?" (Luke 12:14). It was not for this that Jesus came into the world, and his practice of limiting his involvement to the spiritual realm provides a useful example for Christian ministers today.

Furthermore, Jesus was unwilling to aid this man because of his obvious greed. This comes out in his warning to the crowd: "Watch out! Be on your guard against all kinds of greed; a man's life does not consist in the abundance of his possessions" (Luke 12:15). Greed is a lust for things we do not have; it is being discontented with what God has given us. The Bible views greed as incompatible with godliness. Proverbs 21:26 says of the greedy man, "All day long he craves for more, but the righteous give without sparing." Greed is a sin we all have committed, one that constantly brews within our sinful nature. We see why Jesus warned his hearers: "Take heed!" "Be on your guard," or you will be just like this man who, even listening to teaching about the soul, could think only of money.

Jesus followed the warning with a principle that exposes the folly of greed. He said, "A man's life does not consist in the abundance of his possessions" (Luke 12:15). The truth of this is lived out every day. Many people have learned to their sorrow that the family strife caused by an inheritance struggle, like the one this man apparently was waging, is not worth the money. Our generation has been told that "greed is good," but our common experience is that the materialism of our times is anything but a blessing. But this is hardly something novel to our times. A century ago, the British preacher Alexander Maclaren warned his hearers that money does not make the man or the woman:

> Not what we possess, but what we are, is the important matter. . . . The real life of a man has little relation to what he possesses. Neither nobleness nor peace nor satisfaction, nor anything in which man lives a nobler life than a dog, has much dependence on property of any sort. . . . When [greed] has made its pile, it finds that it is no nearer peace of heart, rest, nobleness, or joy than before, and has probably lost much of both in the process of making it. The mad race after wealth, which is the sin of this luxurious, greedy, commercial age, is the consequence of a lie—that life does consist in the abundance of possessions.[1]

In John 17:3, our Lord offered the highest expression of what life is about. Praying to the Father, he said, "Now this is eternal life: that they may know you, the only true God, and Jesus Christ, whom you have sent." The proper life for which we were created consists in the knowledge of God, of fellowship with God, of experiencing the spiritual blessings that come from heaven to his children. The kingdom of God, Paul reminds us, "is not a matter of eating and drinking, but of righteousness, peace and joy in the Holy Spirit" (Rom. 14:17).

In his best-selling novel *The Testament,* John Grisham tells of a multibillionaire who signs a mystery last will just before committing suicide. His children, all of whom have already squandered a small fortune and, like their father, have gained only misery from their money-dominated lives, excitedly gather for the reading of the will. To their shock, the fortune is granted to an unknown, illegitimate daughter of whom none of them have ever heard. This woman, Rachel Lane, had been reared by a minister and his wife and now was a Christian missionary to the indigenous peoples of Brazil. A lawyer, Nate O'Reilly, is promptly dispatched to find her. O'Reilly's lifelong pursuit of riches has resulted in alcoholism, multiple divorce, and estrangement from his children. After much difficulty, the lawyer finally tracks down the missionary, eager to give her the great news that she is the lucky heiress of her unknown father's billions. But in their first meeting, Rachel informs Nate of a different view of life and of money, one that comes from her relationship to Jesus Christ. To the lawyer's disbelief, she flatly turns down the money and refuses to sign any of the documents he has brought. "You worship money, Nate," she explains. "You're part of a culture where everything is measured by money. It's a religion."[2] By her strikingly different attitude toward money, the missionary demonstrated a different kind of life, one that allowed her to minister to the Indians she loved and to the lawyer who came to make her rich but learned of a different kind of riches altogether.

By her example, this fictional character revealed the principle Jesus teaches in Luke 12:15, that life does not consist in the abundance of possessions. This is a lesson Jesus intended to press upon flesh-and-blood men and women. To illustrate his point, he went on to teach a parable. A certain rich man's land produced a great abundance of crops. "He thought to himself, 'What shall I do? I have no place to store my crops" (Luke 12:17). The first thing this shows us is that wealth brings with it great anxiety. J. C. Ryle comments, "The more acres a man has, the more cares. The more his money increases, the more of his time is generally consumed and eaten up in thinking about it."[3] Here we have this man pondering the disposition of his wealth. He is like a father sitting at the breakfast table ignoring his family, anxiously scanning the latest stock quotes, a scene familiar to so many. His money—and especially his longing for more money—causes him the kind of anxiety that keeps people up late into the night.

Possessions, as a rule, do not add to our lives but demand from our lives. How especially true is this in our day than in most, as masses of people groan beneath mounds of credit card debt, as couples work without end to make the mortgage on their luxury home and their luxury cars. How many of us, instead of possessing our goods, are possessed by them!

The rich man in Jesus' parable not only is anxious but also is revealed as exceedingly selfish. Look how many times the word *my* appears in this parable: my crops, my barns, my grain, my goods, myself. This man was undoubtedly surrounded by many people who lived in great poverty. But he thought nothing of them, only of himself. No wonder the parable shows us how isolated the rich man was from others. He has a conversation, but it is only with himself: "He thought to himself." Literally in the Greek it is, "He had a dialogue with himself." Many of us remember the millionaire Howard Hughes, whose life was one of misery and seclusion. This man's behavior points in the same direction, and greed always brings this sad tendency.

Finally, his love of wealth leads him into practical atheism. There is no thought here of God, no prayer for guidance. His land brought forth great abundance, but he does not thank God or attribute his fortune to God's blessing. He assumes the wealth is his without any obligation to God. The decision is his alone, the benefits of his prosperity for him alone. I imagine, if asked, he would have professed to some belief in God, as most people do. Yet this man, like all who share his attitude toward possessions, lived out a practical atheism that was far more real than any words he might say in an infrequent visit to church.

His thoughts bear this out. The rich man had a problem—excess crops—and he arrived at a solution—bigger barns to store them for himself. Luke 12:19 shows his satisfaction at this scheme: "I'll say to myself, 'You have plenty of good things laid up for many years. Take life easy; eat, drink and be merry.'" This is how people think when they believe in no God, no judgment, no life beyond the grave. The apostle Paul used this same expression, writing in 1 Corinthians 15:32 of the hedonism inherent to unbelief: "If the dead are not raised, 'Let us eat and drink, for tomorrow we die.'"

How many people live this way, many of them professing Christians. You can always tell the greedy, practical atheists by the way they live, by their use of time, their casual conversation and interests. All are about money and possessions! If you ask about their goals in life you will hear something like this: "By the time I'm thirty, I'd like to be making a certain salary. By thirty-five I'd like to be a millionaire. I want to be able to retire with great wealth at forty-five." This is living! This is life! The abundance of possessions! You see why Paul warned Christians in Colossians 3:5, "Put to death . . . greed, which is idolatry." No wonder Jesus said to this crowd, "Watch out! Be on your guard against all kinds of greed."

Jesus refers to all such materialists when he says to this rich man, "You fool!" This is not what life is about! This is not what men and women were made for! A craving for money does not lift the soul or satisfy the heart. Indeed, how often wealth creates only an insatiable desire for more wealth. This is what John D. Rockefeller, the great tycoon of a century ago, confessed. When asked, "How much money is enough?" he famously replied, "Just one more dollar." Ecclesiastes 5:10 observes the same: "Whoever loves money never has money enough; whoever loves wealth is never satisfied with his income." How much better we all would do to believe and practice what Paul wrote to Timothy, "Godliness with contentment is great gain" (1 Tim. 6:6). In the thoughts and plans of this foolish rich man in the parable, it is our attitude toward money and success and happiness that comes under his scrutiny. If we see in this rich fool a portrait of ourselves, Jesus wants to turn our attitude toward money and possessions upside down by shining the light of truth upon the reality of our lives.

Your Life Is Demanded!

Jesus called this man a fool because he misunderstood the meaning of life. But this parable also teaches a lesson about false security. This is the second way this rich man worshiped money: first, he made it his life, and second, he saw in it security for the future. Jesus shows God breaking into and ruining his smug glee over his wealth:

> But God said to him, "You fool! This very night your life will be demanded from you. Then who will get what you have prepared for yourself?"
>
> This is how it will be with anyone who stores up things for himself but is not rich toward God. (Luke 12:20–21)

The man believed that by storing up goods he could gain security against an uncertain future. How many people think this way today! The years to come are uncertain; there are risks and dangers. In his folly, this man thinks that by wealth he can control the future. This is because he sees no further than the grave; he sees no judgment or a future beyond death but only "good things laid up for many years." Because of these, he thinks he will "take life easy; eat, drink and be merry."

There are things money can do: it can give you things, it can let you do things, it can stave off certain hardships. But even the greatest pile of money utterly fails as a rampart against death. Maclaren writes, "Death knocks at palaces and poor men's hovels. Millionaires and paupers are huddled together in his net."[4] Not only did this man's riches not safeguard him from death, but also upon his death they will be given to others. "Who will get what you have prepared for yourself?" God asks. "Naked a man comes from his mother's womb, and as he comes, so he departs," says the wise man of Ecclesiastes. "He takes nothing from his labor that he can carry in his hand" (Eccles. 5:15).

An accountant worked for a rich man who had died. A friend asked him, "How much did he leave behind?" "All of it!" he answered. That is the truth about money. It fails to provide happiness even now, and it cannot stave off the real threats of life and especially not of death.

Since death awaits us all, the great question of life is how ready we will be. Since death may come at any moment—as it did for this foolish man—the question becomes, "Are we ready now?" Not only did money fail to secure this man's life, but also the love of money cost him his life. "This very night your life will be demanded from you," God said, and there is here the double sense of handing over his life and of giving an account for it. Leon Morris rightly concludes, "Man whose life hangs by a thread and who may be called upon at any time to give account of himself is a fool if he relies on material things."[5]

Yet how wise such people appear in the eyes of the world. Who is admired but those who strive to get rich, who preach their religion in their houses and cars and lifestyle? Of the lives of the rich and famous the world extols, "How prudent and clever and wise!" But over their graves, God inscribes, "You fool!" Let us therefore pray for the foolish rich, admired in this world. Jesus meant it when he said, "I tell you the truth, it is hard for a rich man to enter the kingdom of heaven" (Matt. 19:23). Let us not envy those whose wealth is accounted only in things. Ryle soberly reminds us, "Poverty has many disadvantages. But riches destroy far more souls than poverty."[6]

The Bible is not against possessions, so long as they are used properly and not in selfish excess. The problem is greed, the love of money. Jesus taught in the Sermon on the Mount: "You cannot serve both God and Money" (Matt. 6:24). How, then, do you stand in those terms? Do you put God first, gratefully receiving from him and living in stewardship to him? Or are you one of those who, despite your words, deny him with your life and like this fool will have an account to give that you will not be able to pay?

Rich toward God

Jesus sums up the point in Luke 12:21, saying, "This is how it will be with anyone who stores up things for himself but is not rich toward God." He contrasts two possible positions, riches in self or riches in God, riches that are worldly or heavenly, that are material or spiritual. Here we have, he says, a sure barometer of our spiritual condition.

One spiritual treasure is faith. James writes, "Has not God chosen those who are poor in the eyes of the world to be rich in faith and to inherit the kingdom he promised those who love him?" (James 2:5). Paul speaks of good deeds as another spiritual treasure, telling Timothy to teach his people "to do good, to be rich in good deeds, and to be generous and willing to share. In this way they will lay up treasure for themselves as a firm foundation for the coming age, so that they may take hold of the life that is truly life" (1 Tim. 6:18–19). William Taylor puts these together as a life rich in God:

> Faith in Jesus Christ enriches us by giving us the blessings of forgiveness, peace, holiness and heaven; and good works, wrought as the outcome of gratitude for these blessings, enrich us with present happiness and future reward. These are things which the world cannot give or take away. These are things which are the possessions of our soul, and of which death cannot deprive us.[7]

In this way a poor man's house, with faith, is richer indeed than the brightest mansion in which God is absent. This combination of faith and works is exactly what we find in the teaching Jesus goes on to give his disciples in the verses that follow. Not surprisingly, his recipe for true riches also contrasts directly with the agenda of earthly riches, exemplified in the case of the rich fool.

Jesus, in teaching on being rich toward God, touches on each aspect of the rich fool's life, turning each aspect upside down through faith in God. We observed that the rich man's great possessions brought anxiety, and Jesus shows that the person who trusts God and not wealth exchanges anxiety for peace. "Therefore I tell you," he says, "do not worry about your life, what you will eat; or about your body, what you will wear. Life is more than food, and the body more than clothes" (Luke 12:22–23). A godly person ought not worry, because if God provides for the ravens, if God dresses the flowers in splendor, then he will provide for all the needs of those who are much more valuable than they. "O you of little faith!" Jesus concludes (Luke 12:28). Riches toward God begin with faith and yield a harvest of peace.

Second, a person who is rich toward God is not selfish, like the rich fool seeking only his own good, but is a seeker of God's kingdom. Instead of chasing the things the world pursues, Christians should "seek [God's] kingdom, and these things will be given to you as well" (Luke 12:31).

According to Jesus, there are two parts to seeking God's kingdom: divesting and investing. We must divest ourselves of the things of the world. Jesus says in Luke 12:33, "Sell your possessions and give to the poor." There has been a great deal of debate regarding how literally this should be taken. All through church history some have taught that salvation literally requires every Christian to have no goods. Often this is modified to exclude normal Christians, while more serious and devout believers, like the monks and nuns, may take on this extra yoke of self-renunciation as a means of gaining superior spiritual benefits. This view is mistaken and harmful, if for no other reason than that people who act like the rich fool are not lower-level Christians. They are not Christians! Whatever Jesus commands here is clearly for all and not merely for some.

The great majority of evangelical commentators argue that Jesus is not demanding the rejection of all material goods. Some interpreters, however, use passages like this to advocate an obligatory kind of Christian communism. But the eighth commandment, "You shall not steal," strongly asserts the right to private property. In one of the great passages condemning greed, Peter's rebuke of Ananias in Acts 5:3–4, that apostle affirms Ananias's right to personal property. "Didn't it belong to you before it was sold?" he asked. "And after it was sold, wasn't the money at your disposal?" In 1 Timothy 5:4–8, Paul commands Christians to provide for the needs of their family members, charging that one who does not scandalizes the faith "and is worse than an unbeliever." Furthermore, Jesus does not say to sell all your possessions. He says, "Sell your possessions and give to the poor" (Luke 12:33).

While avoiding these kinds of unbiblical radicalism, we also must face the true force of Jesus' words. Instead of devoting our lives to acquiring things, Christians are to give generously to others in need. What a difference this change will require and produce in our lives! For one thing, it requires us to cultivate a godly contentment that does not rely on worldly goods. In his timeless classic, *The Rare Jewel of Christian Contentment*, the Puritan Jeremiah Burroughs contrasts the worldly and the godly ways to contentment.

Unlike the man of the world, he says, "A Christian comes to contentment, not so much by way of addition, as by way of subtraction." He explains that the worldly person seeks happiness by acquiring new things to add to what he already has. But for the Christian, Burroughs explains, "Contentment does not come in that way, it does not come, I say, by adding to what you want, but by subtracting from your desires."[8] Christians arrive at contentment not by seeking things they do not yet have but by needing fewer of the things they already have in the goodness of God. This shows how closely tied is our attitude toward money to deep spiritual issues, with much godly gain to those who free themselves from the bondage of greed.

Every Christian should sacrificially restrain his or her acquiring of possessions in order to give more generously to others. If we have never sold or denied ourselves anything in order to give, then in Jesus' terms we are not living a life that is rich toward God. Only by divesting from this world can we safeguard our hearts from the covetousness that is so common and perilous to our spiritual life. Though we now live in the world, we must not be of the world. This requires that we pump the sewage of greed from our hearts the way Noah bilged water from the inside of the ark.

The Christian not only divests from this present age but also invests in the kingdom of God, in the age to come. We say that you can't take riches with you, but here we find that you can indeed send them ahead. This is what Jesus indicates in Luke 12:33: "Provide purses for yourselves that will not wear out, a treasure in heaven that will not be exhausted, where no thief comes near and no moth destroys." As we give and labor and serve for the sake of God's kingdom, in the evangelistic work of the church and in ministering the love of Christ to the world, we not only build up the kingdom of which we ourselves are heirs but also store up treasures in heaven forever. This is what the fictitious Rachel Lane understood and conveyed to her worldly-minded lawyer in *The Testament*. She refused the inheritance of billions because she was storing up treasure of a different, better, and longer-lasting kind. For this reason, the apostle Paul encouraged the Corinthians to excel in this grace, which is most Christ-like above all others—the grace of giving. He wrote, "For you know the grace of our Lord Jesus Christ, that though he was rich, yet for your sakes he became poor, so that you through his poverty might become rich" (2 Cor. 8:9). In this way, Jesus shows us what it means to be rich toward God.

Finally, in contrast to the rich fool's attempt to find security in money, believers must secure themselves in God. Instead of a practical atheism that sees a future only in this life, we are to employ a practical Christianity, a religion that realizes it is our future beyond the grave that truly needs to be secured. Even the uncertain future of our lives in this world is to be placed into God's hands, as we live not for ourselves but for God's kingdom and for the blessing of others. Does this mean that Christians should not have retirement accounts, that we should not save for the education of our children? No, it does not mean that. But there is a difference in attitude that will always reveal itself in our choices and actions. Jesus challenges us, "For where your treasure is, there your heart will be also" (Luke 12:34).

If we Christians must save and invest our money, it should be with a heavy heart for others in need, with an open hand that is still giving generously, and with a Christ-like willingness to sacrifice for the kingdom of God. In our attitude and our actions involving money, the true object of our worship is unfailingly revealed, for where our treasure is there our heart will be found. R. Kent Hughes sums our choice:

> We can enlarge our savings and build huge accounts to hold it all. We can plan our retirement so we will have nothing to do but change positions in the sun. We can plan our menus for the twilight years so that nothing but the finest cuisine crosses our lips. We can live as if this is all of life. We can laugh our way to the grave—only to discover at the end that we have nothing and are in God's eyes fools. Or we can be rich toward God because we gave and gave and gave.[9]

Where is your heart? Is it with yourself or with God? What is your treasure? Is it money and things? Or is your treasure God and his kingdom that lasts forever? Those are questions we answer not with words but with the manner of our lives, in our getting or in our giving. They are practical questions with profound implications. But if we turn to God in faith, seeking grace to change our lives for his sake, we can be sure that he will provide practical solutions that bring true riches to us and glory to his name.

5

The Barren Fig Tree

Luke 13:1–9

A man had a fig tree, planted in his vineyard,
and he went to look for fruit on it, but did not find any.
So he said to the man who took care of the vineyard, "For three
years now I've been coming to look for fruit on this fig tree
and haven't found any. Cut it down! Why should
it use up the soil?" (Luke 13:6–7)

On September 11, 2001, America suffered its greatest tragedy in recent memory, a savage terrorist attack that took thousands of lives on our soil. One result of that tragedy has been a national unity we have seldom known, galvanized by outrage and shared anguish. Another result has been an increase in religious expression, mostly declaring confidence in God's favor toward our nation. We hang signs saying, "God bless America," with the sense it is inevitable that he will. And yet, for all this religious expression, the lessons we have drawn from that tragic day have been mainly military and political; very little is said about the spiritual implications of September 11. But in this passage from Luke chapter 13, Jesus responds to a similar atrocity in his own day with a spiritual observation that has the greatest bearing on our eternal destinies. "Unless you repent," he said, "you will all likewise perish" (v. 5).

A Warning to Repent

Luke 13 begins when Jesus receives a report of an atrocity committed against a group of Jews. Apparently Roman troops had entered the temple on Pontius Pilate's orders and slaughtered a group of Galileans who were making sacrifices there. This is the kind of event that sparks a passion for retaliation. It is the kind of thing that still happens today, and such a report always stirs patriots to a zealous and even murderous rage.

Jesus' hearers had another perspective on the tragedy, one that saw misfortune as a sign of divine disfavor. This accounts for Jesus' reply, "Do you think that these Galileans were worse sinners than all the other Galileans because they suffered this way? I tell you, no!" (Luke 13:2–3). Jesus then reflected on another tragedy that seems to have been fresh in his hearers' minds. The murder in the temple was a violent atrocity, but Jesus adds to it news of a seemingly random accident. A tower had collapsed in Jerusalem, killing eighteen people. Jesus comments, "Do you think they were more guilty than all the others living in Jerusalem? I tell you, no!" (Luke 13:4).

Jesus' attitude toward tragedies like these is strikingly different from that so common to us. So many of us are filled with self-righteous indignation, thinking ourselves vindicated by our cause. Others are relieved they at least were not involved or made victims. Jesus' approach was altogether different. What he said is perhaps shocking to many: "Unless you repent, you too will all perish" (Luke 13:5). That, he said, is what we should realize when disaster strikes. As John Piper has written, Jesus means that "instead of being amazed that sinful humans perish, be amazed that you haven't."[1] News of catastrophe ought to remind us of our mortality, of God's judgment on sin, and then of the guilt that marks us all for condemnation if we do not repent.

When it comes to the matter of our mortality, the September 11 attacks shook most of us. The hijacking of airliners and the destruction of the World Trade Center brought many of us closer to the reality of death than ever before. Especially as we read or heard reports of cell phone conversations from the hijacked airplanes, detailed accounts of those who perished, it was impossible to avoid putting ourselves in their shoes. What would go through our minds if we realized the plane in which we were flying was doomed to destruction? How would we handle the awareness that fire blocked every route of escape a hundred stories above the earth? Many in those situations retained their composure. Some responded with genuine heroism. For a great many their final acts expressed love for family and friends. All this has brought us before the face of death; surely this accounts for much of the resurgence of religious expression we have seen.

But Jesus adds something we have heard little of in all of this, namely, God's judgment on sin. He says to those still living, "Unless you repent, you too will all perish." He tells us that we should learn from tragedies like these that God judges sin. The Greek text makes this a bit clearer, stating, "Unless you repent, you will all likewise perish."

The point is that God's final judgment is like these tragedies—sudden and terrible and violent. John Calvin captures Jesus' thought when he says, "All the calamities that happen in the world are testimonies of the wrath of God."[2] William Arnot explains, "The sudden and unexpected destruction of those sacrificing Galileans, was but an emblem of the sudden and unexpected destruction that would overtake [them] if they were not converted in time, and shielded in mercy from the judgment that sin entailed."[3]

Jesus makes clear that those killed in the tragedies of his day were not more sinful than others, and we must realize that the same is true in our tragedies today. The victims are not singled out because they deserve to suffer and die more than others. The point is that such disasters ought to recall our minds to the reality of judgment to come and the wrath of God on a sinful world. The apostle Peter wrote of this, "The day of the Lord will come like a thief. The heavens will disappear with a roar; the elements will be destroyed by fire, and the earth and everything in it will be laid bare" (2 Peter 3:10).

We must all someday die, and death brings God's judgment (Heb. 9:27). Jesus therefore pointed out the urgent lesson that unless we repent we will perish in that judgment. Repentance is not merely a matter of feeling sorry, nor is it just a matter of confessing sin in some ritual fashion. It is, first, a recognition of our guilt before God. Jesus uses two different words here to describe sinners. First, in Luke 13:2, are sinners, that is, those who transgress the will and law of God. This describes us all, for we all have repeatedly violated God's commandments. The second, in Luke 13:4, translated "guilty," speaks of the debt we owe for what God requires and we have not done. We might think of one as acts of commission and the other as acts of omission, both of which condemn us before God. Repentance means we admit that we are condemned before God for the sins we have committed and for the righteous acts we have failed to do.

Repentance then turns to God for the mercy he offers through his Son, Jesus Christ. Repentance is turning from sin to God, from guilt to grace, from unbelief to faith in Christ, from death to eternal life. This is why repentance and faith are so often spoken of together; really, they are two sides of the same coin. Peter, having described the judgment to come, went on immediately to speak of repentance and faith: "Since everything will be destroyed in this way, what kind of people ought you to be? You ought to live holy and godly lives as you look forward to the day of God" (2 Peter 3:11–12). Jesus announced in Mark 1:15, "The kingdom of God is near. Repent and believe the good news!"

A Call to Bear Fruit

Jesus went on to tell a parable that reinforces what he said in the opening verses. He said, "A man had a fig tree, planted in his vineyard, and he went to look for fruit on it, but did not find any" (Luke 13:6). Luke 13:1–5 tells us how Jesus responded to disaster, but now he tells how we should think in times of peace and calm. Jesus compares us with a fig tree planted in a vineyard and informs us that the owner looks for and expects the presence of fruit.

It was not uncommon for landowners to plant a fig tree in the midst of a vineyard, seeking the plentiful annual fruit of which it was capable. A vineyard was a common biblical metaphor for Israel; Isaiah 5:7 says, "The vineyard of the

LORD Almighty is the house of Israel." Some commentators therefore believe that Jesus is speaking here of the covenant nation Israel, which failed to bear its fruit when it rejected the Messiah. This view is supported by Matthew 21:43, which reflects on the Jews' rejection of Christ, "Therefore I tell you that the kingdom of God will be taken away from you and given to a people who will produce its fruit."

We may also, however, direct Jesus' words to individuals, especially to those in the church. This fig tree was blessed by many advantages in the vineyard. Undoubtedly the ground was selected for its fertility. A vineyard was normally walled and cared for, watered with patient care. Likewise, all of us in the church are taught and prayed for and spiritually encouraged. The Lord therefore looks to us for godly growth. Bearing fruit is the test of our faith, just as it was the test of this fig tree. In Matthew 7:18–20, Jesus said: "A good tree cannot bear bad fruit, and a bad tree cannot bear good fruit. . . . Thus, by their fruit you will recognize them."

God calls you to bear fruit. One way Christians bear fruit is through increasing obedience to God with a growing rejection of sin. This is what Paul meant when he wrote to the Ephesians, "You were once darkness, but now you are light in the Lord. Live as children of light (for the fruit of the light consists in all goodness, righteousness and truth)" (Eph. 5:8–9).

The Bible also speaks of the fruit of the Spirit, the spiritual graces God works into our character. Galatians 5:22–23 says, "The fruit of the Spirit is love, joy, peace, patience, kindness, goodness, faithfulness, gentleness and self-control." These qualities mark a true Christian and validate our profession of faith.

Furthermore, all Christians receive spiritual gifts from the Lord, and we are to bear fruit through their employment in Christian service. Paul writes of this in Colossians 1:10, praying that the believers will "live a life worthy of the Lord and please him in every way: bearing fruit in every good work."

This tells us we are not to live for ourselves. We must live unto God, exerting our energies and resources, spending our time not for our pleasure but for his, for the good of his kingdom and his people, for the glory of his name. Here is the key to the whole Christian life, to know God and live for him. Is there anything more grand, more noble, more exciting and wondrous and filled with joy! We are to live for God and for his pleasure, bearing fruit!

If there is no sign of fruit in your life, then according to Jesus this questions your relationship to him. In a famous passage in John 15, Jesus explained that it is our union with him that gives us power to bear fruit. Fruit, therefore, is the test of our discipleship. "I am the vine," he said, "you are the branches. If a man remains in me and I in him, he will bear much fruit; apart from me you can do nothing. . . . This is to my Father's glory, that you bear much fruit, showing yourselves to be my disciples" (John 15:5–8). Christians are to bear fruit—not by working in our strength, but in the same way a branch bears fruit with the life that comes from and through the vine. We are to look to Christ in faith, being thus connected to him. In that way we can be sure that he will bear his fruit in our lives that are joined to his own.

The Barren Tree Judged

Jesus' parable goes on to show that God judges trees that fail to bear fruit. The owner said to the caretaker, "For three years now I've been coming to look for fruit on this fig tree and haven't found any. Cut it down! Why should it use up the soil?" (Luke 13:7). Here is the stark reality that joins this parable to the earlier conversation. Jesus insisted that calamities teach us to repent or perish, and now he links the idea of repentance to that of bearing fruit—both of which are of urgent importance. This shows us that biblical repentance is more than sad and fleeting emotions but a change of life through faith that goes on to bear new fruit that is pleasing to God.

A bad tree, Jesus says, one that fails to bear fruit, will be cut down so as no longer to use up the soil. This is what John the Baptist declared: "Produce fruit in keeping with repentance." Speaking of God's judgment, he added, "The ax is already at the root of the trees, and every tree that does not produce good fruit will be cut down and thrown into the fire" (Luke 3:8–9). Jesus said the same in John 15:6, "If anyone does not remain in me, he is like a branch that is thrown away and withers; such branches are picked up, thrown into the fire and burned."

Notice that God does this to preserve the well-being of the vineyard, having given ample opportunity for the bad tree to bear fruit. "For three years now I've been coming to look for fruit on this fig tree and haven't found any. Cut it down!" he says. J. C. Ryle applies this as a sober warning to unfaithful Christian churches:

> There is a plain warning here to all professing Churches of Christ. If their ministers do not teach sound doctrine, and their members do not live holy lives, they are in imminent peril of destruction. . . . They may abound in ceremonial religion. They may be covered with the leaves of forms, and services,

> and ordinances. But if they are destitute of the fruits of the Spirit, they are reckoned useless cumberers of the ground. Except they repent, they will be cut down.[4]

The Jewish nation affords a prime example of this. Having rejected Christ, they were cast out of God's vineyard. Another example is the seven churches that received letters from the exalted Lord Jesus in Revelation 2–3. He said to them, "If you do not repent, I will come to you and remove your lampstand from its place" (Rev. 2:5). History records that Christ ultimately removed those churches, and rubble now marks their former places of worship.

But this especially warns believers who give no evidence of the faith they profess. Jesus tells us that our growth as Christians is of vital importance; without it we cannot be saved. Second Peter 1:10–11 says that bearing fruit makes our calling and election sure, not to God but to us. Growth in Christ encourages us that we are joined to him by faith, his life working in our own; it attests our election and ultimate salvation into Christ's eternal kingdom. All of us must see this as a sober warning calling for diligent attention. Those who bear no fruit over time show that whatever their outward appearance, they are not good trees, as Jesus puts it, and God will remove them from his vineyard.

The Time of God's Grace

Jesus' parable does not end there, and that is good news—for if God merely demanded fruit in us, none would measure up to his demands. But Jesus adds the words of the vineyard's caretaker, who protested the destruction of the fruitless fig tree: "Sir," he replied, "leave it alone for one more year, and I'll dig around it and fertilize it. If it bears fruit next year, fine! If not, then cut it down" (Luke 13:8–9).

Many expositors handle these final verses by saying that Jesus Christ, in his saving mercy, is shown interceding for us before the wrathful Father. This is surely not the best interpretation, since it wrongly pits Jesus' mercy against the Father's apparent harshness. But we are saved not because God the Son coerces compassion from an otherwise harsh heavenly Father. Quite to the contrary, the Bible makes clear that it was God the Father whose tender mercy sent his Son on the errand of our salvation. It was because God loved the world that he sent his one and only Son that we might be saved through him (John 3:16).

We do better to view this as God's mercy confronting his justice, which is the tension pictured in the gospel and resolved at the cross of Jesus Christ. There on the cross we see the staggering integrity of God's justice. For when our sins were borne by his precious Son, the one who above all was well-pleasing and beloved to him, God did not shrink back from weighing out the whole measure of his wrath, did not hold back from Jesus one ounce of the judgment due for sin. But there too is God's mercy and love for sinners displayed to the full. For if this is what it took to reconcile his guilty people, God was willing to do it. If this was the price to be paid, the precious blood of God's Son, then God was willing to measure out the full purchase price of our redemption. In this respect the cross is a prism for the fullest possible display of God's glorious attributes—righteousness, truth, justice, joined with mercy and love in the highest. F. F. Bruce comments, "It is in the passion of our Lord that we see the very heart of God laid bare; nowhere is God more fully or more worthily revealed as God than when we see him 'in Christ reconciling the world to himself' (2 Cor. 5:19)."[5]

In the terms of this parable, the effect of this mercy is that there is time for us to repent, believe, and bear fruit, thus escaping the judgment of God. Speaking of the slaughter in the temple and the deaths in the fallen tower, Jesus argued that we should learn to repent in order to escape divine judgment. Here he argues the same from the grace and forbearance of God. What conclusion should we draw from the fact that God's wrath has not yet fallen on a sinful world? What should we think if God has shown his favor? How should our nation respond to the reality that God has blessed America?

Jesus warns that we should not presume upon God's grace but realize that he calls for fruit that is pleasing to him. If God has blessed us individually or as a nation, the right response is to bear fruit befitting repentance and faith, glorifying the God who has shed his grace on us, thus avoiding the wrath that is sure to come in time. According to Christ, the day of grace is temporary; perhaps like the fig tree God will grant to us just one more year. If we do not repent, if we do not bear fruit unto God, we can be sure of what Scripture and history clearly reveal, that God casts aside such people and nations, raising in their place good trees that will bear fruit in his vineyard.

But this parable not only shows God giving extra time. It also portrays the devoted care he provides, the loving ministry of Jesus Christ through his Spirit and the means of grace he has ordained. "I'll dig around it and fertilize it," says the caretaker, and in like fashion, Christ labors for our benefit in this present age of grace in which eternal destinies are fashioned. Think of what God provides for your growth—the teaching of his Word; his grace in the sacrament; the fellowship of believers to exhort and support you, to turn you back from the path of sin; the

Bible for you to read for the renewing of your mind; the regenerating work of the Holy Spirit to revive your will and affections; the great privilege of prayer wherein you may find grace to help you in your time of need (Heb. 4:16) and where you may pray for others and receive the benefits of their prayers for you. We ought to think of the fertilizer the caretaker spreads into the loosened ground as especially referring to the Holy Spirit. Christ sends the Spirit to make fertile the ground of our hearts, which would otherwise be barren. What an encouragement this is! What mercy it is on God's part to work so diligently for our spiritual life, and especially to send his Spirit into our lives!

God is working in your life to bear fruit, if you are joined to Christ. Thus Paul writes in Philippians 2:12–13 that we must work out with fear and trembling the salvation that God gives, "for it is God who works in you," he says, "to will and to act according to his good purpose." So confident is he of the fruitfulness of everyone who truly believes that he assures us, "He who began a good work in you will carry it on to completion until the day of Christ Jesus" (Phil. 1:6).

This parable gives us a similar perspective on the trials the Lord brings into our lives. Luke 13:8 shows the caretaker using fertilizer to impart vitality to the weak tree but also "digging around it" to loosen the soil. Similarly God employs hardships and trials to loosen our hold on this world, to make room for his grace to win through to our hearts. Peter said of trials: "These have come so that your faith—of greater worth than gold, which perishes even though refined by fire—may be proved genuine and may result in praise, glory and honor when Jesus Christ is revealed" (1 Peter 1:7). William Arnot observes,

> The Lord who pours in the food for the sustenance of the soul, stirs that soul by his providence, so that grace may reach the root and be taken in. . . . It is when afflictions rend the heart, as a ploughshare tears up the ground, that the elements of life long offered are at length received. It is thus that providence and grace conspire to achieve the purpose of God in the salvation of men.[6]

God does not merely provide a space of time to see which trees will bear fruit, but he actively works in his people's hearts to bring them to fruitful life, as well as to learn firsthand of the bad trees that remain barren. Ultimately he will cut down the barren tree for his good and for the good of the vineyard as well.

That You May Bear Much Fruit

What a great incentive for us to persevere in the hardships of the Christian life, to turn to God in faith that he would make us grow and bear fruit. Yet what a warning to those who presume upon his grace, refusing to repent and remaining spiritually barren. God's kindness to any people is intended to evoke repentance and new life through faith. Paul warns in Romans 2:4, "Do you show contempt for the riches of his kindness, tolerance and patience, not realizing that God's kindness leads you toward repentance?" In blessing and calamity, we are called by Christ to respond with the same mind, as he announced at the outset of his ministry: "The time has come," he said. "The kingdom of God is near. Repent and believe the good news!" (Mark 1:15).

Do you realize that the great matters of faith and life are ever the same? What is the great problem of this world but sin—sin that brings God's wrath and ruins his creation? What is the remedy in every individual's or nation's life, the great issue that defines eternal destinies, but repentance to the Lord in faith? And what is the purpose for our redemption, but that we should bear fruit that is pleasing to God? This is the whole pattern of the Christian life in every generation. It is the pattern of God's whole redemptive work in this world and the yardstick by which we may assess every endeavor, every life, every individual who claims to know the Lord. Jesus said, "This is to my Father's glory, that you bear much fruit, showing yourselves to be my disciples" (John 15:8).

Surely this is the lesson God would have us consider now—individually and together as a nation. Let us continue to cry, "God bless America." But let us turn it around from a claim or demand to a prayerful plea. Let us turn our hearts from a vindicating self-righteousness to a repentant cry for grace. May God indeed bless America, most of all with grace to admit our guilt and shame, repenting in faith to serve the Lord anew. "This is to my Father's glory," taught our Lord, "that you bear much fruit, showing yourselves to be my disciples" (John 15:8).

The Mustard Seed and Yeast

Luke 13:18–21

Then Jesus asked, "What is the kingdom of God like? What shall I compare it to? It is like a mustard seed, which a man took and planted in his garden. It grew and became a tree, and the birds of the air perched in its branches." (Luke 13:18–19)

Many centuries ago, a young religious figure gathered a small group of students and began traveling the country teaching the people and doing good deeds. Reports had it that he performed miracles. Among the poor and disenfranchised many attached to him great hopes for revolution. Accordingly the religious leaders of the day went out to investigate. They found that while he attracted great crowds, his enigmatic teaching often left them puzzled. His group of committed followers seemed quite small, a dozen or so men and a small group of women. What troubled them most was his apparent disrespect for established conventions. In particular, this teacher infuriated them by continuing with his ministry on the day of the week set aside for rest. When they confronted him with this breach of conduct, the teacher publicly assaulted their authority, declaring the religious leaders hypocrites.

The upstart teacher seems to have realized how troubling this might be to his small band of followers. They believed he was the Messiah who would bring God's divine kingdom to the earth. But, despite his popularity, his ministry did not seem to increase in terms of any tangible sources of influence. Furthermore, his conflict with the rulers only got worse as time went by, casting a threatening cloud over their hopes for a sweeping, national success. Therefore the teacher, whose name was Jesus of Nazareth, told a parable to explain how they should understand what was happening. "What is the kingdom of God like?" he began. "What shall I compare it to? It is like a mustard seed, which a man took and planted in his garden. It grew and became a tree, and the birds of the air perched in its branches."

Big Things from Small Beginnings

The point of this picture is obvious, namely, that things with small beginnings can end up quite significant and large. The mustard seed was proverbial for its extreme smallness; each seed was barely a millimeter long. Evidence suggests that the rabbis used it as a symbol for something imperceptible and tiny. Luke records Jesus doing just that on another occasion: "If you have faith as small as a mustard seed," he said, "you can say to this mulberry tree, 'Be uprooted and planted in the sea,' and it will obey you" (Luke 17:6).

From its small beginning, the mustard seed produces a shrublike plant that grows to an astounding size, in some cases as large as nine or even twelve feet high. On the branches of what started out so small, flocks of birds perch in the shade and eat. The parable therefore combines the idea of something large arising from what was very small with the concept of powerful growth.

The kingdom of God is his saving rule, his work of grace and righteousness, the administration of his will among his people. Jesus taught us to pray, "Your kingdom come, your will be done." Those two always go together. And yet the kind of things the Jewish people associated with God's kingdom were conspicuously absent in Jesus' ministry—things like military power, national triumph, and visible glory. Instead, the disciples should understand the presence of God's kingdom in this world as a mustard seed that produces a great tree. Jesus' ministry, though apparently so small, marked the beginning of something great; it was the seed that contains the whole tree in its growth.

This teaching is borne out in the history of the church. How feeble and helpless the early Christians appeared, yet they overcame and spread and grew into a great tree. In its branches many have found safety and rest. The Anglican bishop J. C. Ryle expressed this most eloquently, saying of Christianity:

> Its first founder was One who was poor in this world, and ended His life by dying the death of a malefactor on the cross. Its first adherents were a lit-

> tle company, whose number probably did not exceed a thousand when the Lord Jesus left the world. Its first preachers were a few fishermen and publicans, who were, most of them, unlearned and ignorant men. Its first starting point was a despised corner of the earth, called Judea, a petty tributary province in the vast empire of Rome. Its first doctrine was eminently calculated to call forth the enmity of the natural heart. Christ crucified was to the Jews a stumbling block, and to the Greeks foolishness. . . . If ever there was a religion which was a little grain of seed at its beginning, that religion was the Gospel.

That is how Christianity began, yet from that start came amazing growth, the little seed spreading with the power of God for the salvation of those who believed. Ryle concludes:

> Year after year its adherents became more numerous. Year after year idolatry withered away before it. City after city, country after country, received the new faith. . . . In a few hundred years, the religion of the despised Nazarene, the religion which began in the upper chamber at Jerusalem, had overrun the civilized world. . . . The grain of mustard seed "waxed a great tree; and the fowls of the air lodged in the branches of it."[1]

Some people believe that this parable teaches a continuous spread of Christianity that will one day literally fill the earth, finally eradicating all false, competing faiths. This is the view known as postmillennialism, which sees Christ returning only after the church has evangelized and discipled the whole earth. This parable is the classic text in support of that view. Other passages, however, indicate this interpretation takes its message too far. In the parable of the weeds, for instance, which accompanies this parable in Matthew's Gospel, Jesus says that there will always be weeds growing alongside the wheat, and only after Jesus returns will the weeds be pulled up and the church purified. Therefore we should stop short of teaching a continuous progress that will inexorably lead to worldwide conversion prior to Christ's return. What the parable mainly relates is a small beginning and a great ending, which the Bible elsewhere teaches will take place after and not before Christ's return (see Matt. 13:29–30; 2 Thess. 2:5–8). The parable of the mustard seed teaches a glorious consummation without giving details about how it comes. Its point is that something very small, with the right power, can grow and grow and grow.

What is true in the grand scale of the history of our faith is also true of all its great movements. The Protestant Reformation began as a small seed in the hearts of men like Martin Luther and Huldrich Zwingli. Luther sought personal assurance of salvation, wearying the Catholic priests with hours of confession. On the advice of his mentor he searched the Scripture, and there he found the gospel of justification through faith alone. His first public act was to nail his Ninety-five Theses to a castle church door. What could be smaller than that! When the pope first heard of it, he exclaimed that Luther was a drunken German monk. "When he sobers up, it will all be over," he remarked. But it was not over, for in Luther's message of justification through faith in Christ, God's kingdom was unleashed and began to grow. In the year 2000, polls were taken as to the most important influential people of the previous thousand years, and many scholars agreed that nothing happened in the last millennium more powerful or important than the Reformation. What began in such smallness, as a single monk discovered the gospel, had a great result indeed.

The history of revivals reveals the same phenomenon. In 1815, Robert Haldane visited Geneva, Switzerland. One day he was sitting in the park reading his Bible, when he met some students from the theological academy. He soon realized that these seminarians had no understanding of the gospel, so he invited them to come to his rooms for a Bible study twice a week. Haldane led them through Paul's Book of Romans and one after another the students were converted. That seems a small thing. But those few students went on to lead the revivals that spread all through France in the years to follow, a movement that was given the Scotsman's name, Haldane's Revival.

Let me give one further example that involves simple Christian people. In July 1857 a businessman named Jeremiah Lanphier was appointed an evangelist by his New York City church. Lanphier handed out notices for a noonday prayer meeting every Wednesday. That first week he nervously waited for people to show up. A half hour passed before anyone appeared. Finally, six people came to pray that noonday. It was not much of a beginning, but through the faith and prayers of this man and the others, the kingdom of God was planted and began to grow. The next week twenty came, and then forty. At this point they decided to hold daily meetings.

During that time a remarkable event took place, a financial panic that swept the country and ruined the economy. In its wake, Christian revivals were reported across America and Canada. In New York, more people came to

Lanphier's prayer meeting, and the number of conversions grew. By February of the next year, the prayer meeting had grown to a prayer movement spread all over New York City. Evangelical ministers were brought in to teach and preach the gospel. One historian says, "Within six months of that first Fulton Street meeting, 10,000 businessmen were gathering daily in New York City for prayer, and within two years a million converts had been added to the American churches," through this and other revivals.[2]

You see how this parable challenges our thinking. We find it hard to believe that small and weak beginnings can lead to something great. But when it is the kingdom of God that is planted, that small beginning contains within it a great destiny. God's kingdom is planted when a man or woman comes to faith in Christ; when God moves a believer to become earnest in Bible study or prayer, in witness or in works; when God convicts a minister to faithfully preach the gospel; when God convicts a church to faithfully and seriously attend the preaching of the Word. God does not always use these to bring about mass revivals or historical reformations, although he can and sometimes does. But every humble beginning of God's kingdom, unnoticed or scorned by the world, has within it power from God for great and mighty works of salvation, with results that last forever.

What a difference this makes to a Christian struggling in difficulty! Even a small amount of grace from God is as the mustard seed to the tree, growing by his power. Many a minister labors under apparent failure, with little response to his faithful preaching of God's Word. But our Lord assures him that the planting of his seeds will bear godly fruit in time. A Christian struggles in a ministry where growth is slow and progress is scarce. But in this parable our Lord Jesus promises that no Christian wastes his or her time in the planting of even something so small as a mustard seed for the sake of God's kingdom. Indeed, if we want to see revival or other great works of God, this teaching tells us there is no other way for us to begin than by obedience in small things. It is always through the preaching and the study of the Bible, through prayer, through following the leading of the Holy Spirit as God works in our individual hearts that great things in God's kingdom are begun.

Pervasive and Penetrating Power

One reason why God's kingdom grows is that the gospel's influence is penetrating and pervasive. This is the point of the second parable Jesus added to that of the mustard seed. Luke 13:20–21 tells us, "Again he asked, 'What shall I compare the kingdom of God to? It is like yeast that a woman took and mixed into a large amount of flour until it worked all through the dough.' "

Here Jesus turns to a most common occurrence in his time, the preparation of bread, the staple food of the people. Baking bread required the use either of yeast, which is a fermenting fungus, or of leaven. The word in our passage is better translated as "leaven," which was a piece of fermented dough from the previous baking that would be mixed into the new batch of dough. Just a little leaven would be worked through the whole batch, and that would make the loaf rise when baked. What the New International Version translates as "a great deal of flour" is in the Greek "three satas." That is an enormous amount, flour to make forty loaves of bread. Just like leaven, Jesus says, even a little of the gospel works and penetrates powerfully in the world.

Many commentators point out that Scripture generally uses leaven as a symbol for evil. The Jews sanctified themselves by eating unleavened bread. Paul referred to sin as yeast, which "works through the whole batch of dough" (1 Cor. 5:6). In Luke 12:1, Jesus spoke against "the yeast of the Pharisees, which is hypocrisy." Some expositors, especially those committed to a premillennial view of church history, therefore view this parable as teaching an advancing corruptness in the church. But that teaching does not seem to fit the point Jesus is making here. The distinguishing feature of leaven is its pervasive or infiltrating power, a point that can be applied to either good or evil. In this case, it is hard to see how a negative interpretation fits alongside the parable of the mustard seed, which ends so positively. Therefore a more balanced view of this parable is one given by Arland Hultgren. Jesus' teaching is, he says, that "though hidden in the present, the kingdom will transform the whole of creation, just as leaven transforms flour."[3]

Leaven pervades the dough and makes it rise. In the same way the gospel penetrates the lives of all who believe, spreading and extending its influence until finally, in glory, Christians will be like Christ (Rom. 8:29). How futile it is, then, to try to contain its sphere of activity in our lives. People find their hearts gripped by the message of the crucified Jesus Christ, but they want to keep his influence away from their place of work, out of their social circle, away from the petty sins they have grown to cherish. But it is impossible to restrain the growth of the kingdom of God, once it is rooted within, just as it is impossible to remove or contain the leaven that is placed inside the dough. If it is a true work of grace that is rooted in your heart, you will not contain it in a corner of your life. It will spread and shape in Christ's image your dreams, your goals, your affections, your leisure, your manner of speaking, your habits, your relationships, your use of money, your whole way of thinking and living—all of which will be laid at the feet of the Savior Jesus Christ and transformed by God's marvelous grace.

Does this knowledge that God's grace is like yeast make you afraid to begin or proceed in the gospel of Jesus Christ? Let me assure you that while God intends for you things you would never choose for yourself—at least at the beginning of your Christian life—his intentions for you are all holy and good. His is a kingdom of light and joy and peace and holy love. God works these into your life, as his kingdom takes over and animates more of your existence, and it is all for your good and his glory. Since even a little grace works this way, no godly influence is ever wasted and no beginning of grace is ever too small. Even the weakest soul may know that what God begins he will also complete. Paul writes, "He who began a good work in you will carry it on to completion until the day of Christ Jesus" (Phil. 1:6).

God's grace affects society in the same way it affects individuals. What happens when the gospel grips a great many people and God's Word becomes an open force in a city or nation, school or workplace? We find the answer in this parable of the leaven. God's kingdom spreads and causes the whole to rise.

Perhaps the best example of this comes from Geneva in the time of the great Reformer John Calvin. Calvin had fled the city of Paris, where he was converted to the evangelical faith and had written in its defense. When persecution broke out, Calvin headed for Italy, where there were safe havens and where he hoped to continue his scholarship. However, the movements of armies blocked his path, forcing Calvin to detour in Geneva. There he was recognized and somewhat against his wishes was enlisted as a preacher. That was Calvin's small beginning that would so greatly influence history.

In 1535, Geneva made its break with Catholicism and joined the Protestant Reformation. The civic leaders were motivated by a desire to clean up the infamously low state of morals in their city. Calvin soon arrived, and his preaching at first made little impact. He was so unnoticed by the rulers that they forgot to pay him in that first year. By 1538, Calvin's preaching of God's Word had become so unpopular that he was dismissed, and he happily retreated to the more pleasant city of Strasbourg. But things eventually got so much worse in Geneva that the people called him back. Let me allow James Montgomery Boice to finish the story, one that shows how powerful is God's Word on an entire people:

> Calvin had no weapon but the Bible. From the very first, his emphasis had been on Bible teaching, and he returned to it now, picking up precisely where he had left off three and a half years earlier. Calvin preached from the Bible every day, and under the power of that preaching the city began to be transformed. As the people of Geneva acquired knowledge of God's Word and were changed by it, the city became, as John Knox called it later, a New Jerusalem from which the gospel spread to the rest of Europe, England and the New World.[4]

We often hear how pointless and foolish is the mere preaching of the Bible. Yet among the practical effects of Calvin's preaching was a drastic improvement in the health of Geneva's citizens through the establishment of sanitary standards and the erection of a hospital and poorhouse.

Calvin founded the famous and influential Academy. He urged the introduction of the cloth and silk industries to provide a stable economy, which was fueled by the Bible's emphasis on honesty and hard work. So pervasive were the effects of God's kingdom through Calvin's teaching of the Word that one historian observes, "It is no mere coincidence that religious and political liberty arose in those countries where Calvinism had penetrated most deeply."[5]

At the return of Jesus Christ, what is true of the leaven in the dough will be true of all creation as every square inch of the cosmos will be reclaimed to the service of God. Revelation 11:15 looks forward to that time when "the kingdom of the world has become the kingdom of our Lord and of his Christ, and he will reign for ever and ever." Then, as Isaiah foresaw, God's kingdom will be so pervasive that "the earth will be full of the knowledge of the LORD as the waters cover the sea" (Isa. 11:9). How penetrating and pervasive is the power of God's kingdom!

Hidden Glory and Might

Finally, both of these parables show God's kingdom as a power that is hidden in this world. In Luke 13:19, Jesus says the mustard seed is "planted" or "buried" in a garden. We find this more clearly yet in Luke 13:21, where in the Greek the woman literally "hides" the leaven within the flour. In this manner, God's kingdom, which brings with it the promise of growth and of permeating power, is nonetheless invisible to the eyes of the world.

So much of what is true of every believer is hidden from the world, and even from ourselves. We are not draped with priestly robes, whiter than snow. We bear no visible regalia as proof of God's love for us. We go through this world without hosts of angels audibly proclaiming us heirs of heaven with Christ. Hugh Martin adds, "Nor do the forests clap their hands at our approach, nor the mountains and the hills break forth before us singing in welcome to the sons and heirs of the King of Glory. Rather, the whole creation groans because our sonship is hidden, waiting for the manifestation of it. A cross lies heavy on our shoulder, rather than a diadem shining on our head."[6] All our possessions in Christ are like the seed within the ground, the yeast within the dough, powerful but unseen. Only by faith do we see what is otherwise hidden, great truths like that written by John in his first epistle: "How great is the love the Father has lavished on us, that we should be called children of God! And that is what we are!" (1 John 3:1).

How much more was all this true in the earthly ministry of our Lord. This is why Christ's disciples could not take comfort in worldly riches or power or glory, because Christ's kingdom is one of hidden power received by faith. What was Jesus but a poor man, a carpenter's son, estranged from the power brokers, soon to be crushed beneath authority's boot? But what eyes could not behold, what was hidden to all but those who looked in faith, was the great truth that here was God's own and only Son. Here was Godhood veiled in flesh, incarnate deity! Hidden in Christ and in his gospel was the kingdom of God, which in time will return upon the clouds of heaven with, as Daniel saw, "authority, glory and sovereign power." Here in his humble servant ministry was "an everlasting dominion that will not pass away, a kingdom . . . that will never be destroyed" (Dan. 7:14).

God's kingdom was especially hidden by the cross on which our Savior died. Here is the great mystery on which the gospel is founded, that in the weakness and defeat of his death Jesus established God's kingdom with all-conquering power. There he gained the victory over sin and death, so that all who trust in him might be reconciled to God through the forgiveness of our sin. Hidden in the darkness of his death is found the light of the world for all who believe that Jesus Christ is Savior and Lord.

It may seem like a small thing for you to believe in Jesus. Small the way a mustard seed is small, bringing with it an eternal destiny in glory. Faith in the gospel may seem insignificant, but like a little leaven hidden in a batch of flour it will change everything in your life. Believing that Jesus is God's Son who lived and died and rose again for you may produce results that are invisible to the eyes of the world—things like righteousness, peace, and joy. But in the world to come, our union with Christ will be revealed in all its saving splendor. Jesus said, "I tell you, whoever acknowledges me before men, the Son of Man will also acknowledge him before the angels of God" (Luke 12:8). The seed becomes a tree, the leaven powerfully works and spreads, and what now is hidden will then be revealed. Such is the kingdom of God, and so it will be for all who enter by the way that is Christ.

The Great Banquet

Luke 14:15–24

Blessed is the man who will eat at the feast in the kingdom of God. (Luke 14:15)

Jesus' parable of the great banquet in Luke 14 takes place at the house of a Pharisee, where Jesus as usual was being scrutinized by the religious leaders. The air was tense if not combative. It was a Sabbath day, and seeing that one of the guests had an illness Jesus healed him. Afterward, he challenged the Pharisees to rule on what he had done. At this the conversation turned sour, Jesus not having observed the rule against talking politics or religion in a social setting. This reminds us how undomesticated our Lord is. He chastised them for entertaining only rich friends and family while excluding the poor, the crippled, the lame, the blind.

Probably wanting to change the subject, a man near Jesus interjected a banal and pious aphorism. Luke 14:15

records it: "When one of those at the table with him heard this, he said to Jesus, 'Blessed is the man who will eat at the feast in the kingdom of God.' " Some writers think he was trying to draw something provocative out of Christ. If so, Jesus gratified him with this parable of the great banquet.

The Great Banquet

Many of Jesus' parables are difficult to understand, but this one is remarkably straightforward. The parable teaches five points, beginning with Jesus' depiction of God's kingdom as a great banquet. "A certain man was preparing a great banquet and invited many guests," he began, playing off of the setting in which they were gathered (Luke 14:17). Salvation life in the kingdom of God, Jesus agreed, is a feast for those who are invited and who also come.

Do you ever think about how great it is to be a Christian, what a feast it is to be child of God and citizen of heaven? The Bible says that if by faith we have Christ, then we have all things. Paul said in Romans 8:32, "He who did not spare his own Son, but gave him up for us all—how will he not also, along with him, graciously give us all things?" In Ephesians 1:3, Paul sings out a whole chorus of blessings from Christ's banquet table. "Praise be to the God and Father of our Lord Jesus Christ," he begins, "who has blessed us in the heavenly realms with every spiritual blessing in Christ." He lists some of these blessings in that chapter: election, adoption, redemption, forgiveness, fulfillment in Christ—this is the portion of all who come to God through faith in Christ. J. C. Ryle writes of this bounty:

> The Gospel contains a full supply of everything that sinners need in order to be saved. . . . Forgiveness of

> all sin, and peace with God; justification of the person, and sanctification of the heart; grace by the way, and glory in the end. . . . Christ, in one word, is the sum and substance of the "great supper." "I am the bread of life," He declares, "He that comes to me shall never hunger, and he that believes on me shall never thirst" (John 6:35).[1]

Compare with this the sad fare of the unbeliever, who has no such table spread before him. On what does he feed his soul but the things of this world? Do you ever wonder why so many rich people are unhappy? Counting money and fondling possessions are no feast for the soul! Do you know why so many love relationships turn sour, marriage so often turning to divorce? No sinful human being is ever qualified to play the role of savior for another. Are you surprised that people find work so unfulfilling, their career ambitions turning to hollow despair? Is not our constant, frenzied pursuit of recreation a sign of an emptiness within? The simple truth is that the stuff of earth provides no banquet for humanity, which was made for eternity.

But the truths upon which a Christian feeds are food for the soul indeed. Christians look upon the past and ponder there God's electing love from even before creation. They see God's Son coming to live and die and rise again for their salvation. What a feast that is for the meditation of the mind and the filling of the soul! Christians also own the present as a feast, even in trials, for the Spirit of the living God dwells and moves within us. In times of celebration, we know we are partaking of eternal joys to come, not a fleeting happiness. In times of trouble or distress, Christians have God as a mighty fortress for security, peace, and hope. Especially Christians own the future, and they know that there awaits for them a heavenly feast of which no human mind can conceive, prepared for them by God. The banquet we now enjoy through faith pales compared with the feast God has laid in store for heaven. "Blessed are those who are invited to the wedding supper of the Lamb!" says the angel at the end of days, in Revelation 19:9.

Invitation Only

The second point Jesus makes is that entry into this feast is by invitation only. In the ancient world two invitations would be sent out, one in advance to which the equivalent of RSVPs would be returned, and then another notifying the guests that the feast was prepared and was ready to begin. We see this in Luke 14:16–17: "A certain man was preparing a great banquet and invited many guests. At the time of the banquet he sent his servant to tell those who had been invited, 'Come, for everything is now ready.' "

That raises the vital question about God's kingdom feast—have you received an invitation? Before we come to an answer, let's reflect on how important the issue is. If God does not invite you into eternal life, if God has nothing prepared for you in heaven, what can you do? If God has no victory over death into which he invites you, what possible remedy can you concoct? The problems of life and death are too great for humankind to solve; however much progress we claim to make, the age-old problems of hatred, violence, dishonesty, selfishness, not to mention the mortality of our flesh, remain unsolved and essentially unchanged. Life as it is contains no feast. That is why atheistic philosophy necessarily leads us into the dark arms of despair. Let me quote a current skeptic, who is honest about facing life without the hope that comes from God:

> The whole conviction of my life now rests upon the belief that the sense of loneliness, far from being a rare and curious phenomenon peculiar to myself and to a few other solitary people, is the central and inevitable fact of human existence. All this hideous doubt, despair, and dark confusion of the soul a lonely person must know, for he is united to no image save that which he creates himself.[2]

Without an invitation from God, without a portal out from the closed realm of our finite, death-bound existence, the reflective soul is left with this. Without an invitation from God for something more, we must choose between delusion or despair, the latter of which the skeptic above chose as the more honest of the two.

So I ask the question again, "Is there an invitation from God to something more than meets the eye, to something beyond this life, to a banquet feast in his kingdom?" Jesus says there is. He says that invitations were sent out long before, and now that he has come, the Son of God in flesh, the call goes forth to come to a table that is set.

This summarizes the message of the Old Testament, and especially of the prophets, who sent out the advance invitation to the banquet God would prepare through his Son. Isaiah 55:1–3 says, "Come, all you who are thirsty, come to the waters; and you who have no money, come, buy and eat! Come, buy wine and milk without money and without cost. . . . Eat what is good, and your soul will delight in the richest of fare . . . that your soul may live." A few verses later Isaiah explains the spiritual meaning of this invitation: "Seek the LORD while he may be found; call on him while he is near. Let the wicked forsake his way and the evil man his thoughts. Let him turn to the LORD, and he will have mercy on him, and to our God, for he will freely pardon" (Isa. 55:6–7).

That was the advance call that had gone out to Israel, to the honored guests like the Pharisees who sat at the table with Jesus. They had sent in their RSVPs, but with Jesus' coming the banquet now was prepared. The Pharisee glibly spoke of the feast of God's kingdom, but in Jesus' coming the banquet was ready for all who would come.

Who does Jesus invite? He invites all the weary: "Come to me, all you who are weary and burdened, and I will give you rest" (Matt. 11:28). He invites all whose hearts are dry and empty: "If anyone is thirsty, let him come to me and drink. Whoever believes in me, . . . streams of living water will flow from within him" (John 7:37–38). Jesus invites those guilty of sin: "I have not come to call the righteous, but sinners" (Mark 2:17). All are invited, whoever will come, for Jesus says in John 6:37, "Whoever comes to me I will never drive away."

Revealing Excuses

God in his grace invites all to his table, and thus none can say they were not asked. Yet Jesus' parable shows that many will not come, despite their invitation. This is our third point, that many reject God's invitation with feeble excuses. Jesus continued, "He sent his servant to tell those who had been invited, 'Come, for everything is now ready.' But they all alike began to make excuses" (Luke 14:17–18). This is the reception the gospel continually receives wherever it falls upon the ears of people. Multitudes do this even today. Christ invites them, but they will not come. And why not? Jesus gives three illustrative cases.

First, he tells of man who said, "I have just bought a

field, and I must go and see it. Please excuse me" (Luke 14:18). Here is one whose possessions are in the way of accepting God's invitation. He has much to do with this land he now owns. He must gaze upon it, plan out its use, situate the crops, and position the buildings. He is sorry, he would like to come, but his possessions will not let him wait. Many are like this today. Jesus earlier had taught, "Where your treasure is, there your heart will be also" (Luke 12:34). The man's choice revealed what he thinks most substantial and most attractive, his plot of land or fellowship with God.

Few deny the value of religion, yet many plead the unfortunate duty, indeed the necessity, of forsaking God and his heavenly banquet for the sake of their worldly goods and fortunes. In reality, it is nothing but their hostility to God and disdain for his will that motivates this poor choice that will leave them impoverished in the end.

Next, Jesus gives the excuse of a man who has his career and worldly duties to think about. "Another said, 'I have just bought five yoke of oxen, and I'm on my way to try them out. Please excuse me' " (Luke 14:19). Here we have ambition standing between men and women and their relationship with God. Marcus Dods remarks, "Of how many men in their prime does this man stand as the representative; men so engrossed in the business or pursuits of the world that they positively do not know that God has any claims upon their time—so busy in pushing forward mercantile or scientific or literary or political or military affairs, that it never once occurs to them that there are other objects for the sake of which these affairs should be for a time suspended." All these endeavors, he explains, "are but as the five yoke of oxen when compared with that closest intercourse with God to which we are invited."[3]

Charles Spurgeon tells of a ship owner who was asked by a Christian, "Well, sir, what is the state of your soul?" The businessman replied, "Soul? I have no time to take care of my soul. I have enough to do just taking care of my ships." But, Spurgeon concludes, the man was not too busy to die, and die he did just a week later.[4]

Third, Jesus presents the case of one who puts his earthly relationships ahead of God. "Still another said, 'I just got married, so I can't come' " (Luke 14:20). Later in this chapter, Jesus renders his verdict on this excuse: "If anyone comes to me and does not hate his father and mother, his wife and children, his brothers and sisters—yes, even his own life—he cannot be my disciple. And anyone who does not carry his cross and follow me cannot be my disciple" (Luke 14:26–27).

The bottom line in all three of these cases is indifference to God, to salvation, to the spiritual things in life. Behind the thin veneer of their excuses was a belief that they had better offers elsewhere. There were more exciting and more profitable engagements than that offered at this feast. Let this be a warning to all who put worldly things before the things of God. Your choice reveals an enmity to God, a distaste for the things of heaven, and unless you repent you will give a fatal affront to the King of heaven, in whose hand your eternal destiny lies.

Therefore let no one who refuses God's invitation complain when God neglects your care in the trials of this life and especially in the testing time of death. In Luke 14:24, Jesus shows the rejected host's anger: "I tell you, not one of those men who were invited will get a taste of my banquet." The Pharisees, like the man who flippantly spoke of God's blessed feast, were of course the targets of Jesus' parable. For all their pious talk, they spurned God's feast in the person of Jesus Christ, and they would be rejected by God in return.

Bring Them In!

We all know what it is like to plan a big party, send out invitations, prepare the food, clean and decorate, and then anxiously wait to see if anybody is going to show up. Imagine the heartache of this host who is spurned by his guests. Yet according to Jesus when this happens to God, he does not sulk in failure. Here is how he responds:

> The servant came back and reported this to his master. Then the owner of the house became angry and ordered his servant, "Go out quickly into the streets and alleys of the town and bring in the poor, the crippled, the blind and the lame." (Luke 14:21)

This parable not only warns those who spurn God but also gives a moving portrayal of God's generous grace. Here we find that God's purpose in salvation is not thwarted by unwilling men and women, that his banquet table is filled by others who take their place. This is our fourth point, and it shows in action the wonderful principle stated by Paul in Romans 5:20, "Where sin increased, grace increased all the more." All of the enmity of sinners is overmatched by the grace of God that brings many to the table of salvation.

What an incentive this is for the evangelistic work of the gospel. "Go out into the streets and alleys of the city," God commands. "Go into the countryside, along the lanes and through the hedges to bring them in!" "Make them come," he cries, inciting our zeal in persuasion, in example, in prayer, in persistence of appeal. Indeed, Jesus more than hints at God's compulsive will, the effectual call of his gospel when accompanied by the regenerating work of the Holy Spirit. The three examples of those who made excuses shows that none will be brought unwillingly, yet it is God's irresistible grace that makes us willing, compelling us sweetly with bonds of love, putting the words of faith upon our lips, the cry for grace within our hearts.

Luke 14:22 makes a marvelous addition to this portrait of God's free salvation offer to the world. The servant brought in all the poor of the city but still exclaimed, "Sir, what you ordered has been done, but there is still room." Ryle writes that this "seems to show that there is more willingness on God's part to save sinners, than there is on the part of sinners to be saved, and more grace to be given, than there are hearts willing to receive it."[5] What matters to us, with grace abounding like this for all who will come, is that we should not remain outside, that we should not heed the excuses of our sinful hearts, and that we should not stay outside when God has prepared so sumptuous a feast for those who believe.

Glory to the King!

Our fifth point deals with those brought in to enjoy the banquet the others had spurned. It might seem that God's banquet is dishonored by the absence of the high and the mighty and the presence of "the poor, the crippled, the blind and the lame," as Jesus describes them in Luke 14:21, along with those from the country brought in from far away. We might put these new guests into two groups, the lowly and the lost. Notice that God is ashamed of neither, that with them at his table God is glorified and not disgraced, he is pleased and not embarrassed. This is the fifth point, that the poor and the lost improve this feast and that through them God is exalted in the highest.

The Pharisees, who held these classes of people in contempt, would never think of inviting them to a banquet. They looked down on all "the poor, the crippled, the blind and the lame." As for those found in distant regions, Jesus probably has the Gentiles in mind, and the thought of Gentiles entering God's salvation was unthinkable to the Pharisees. In their mind, the host in the parable had disgraced himself by the lowly company he had brought to his table.

Jesus' attitude was completely different. He began his ministry by identifying just such people as the special objects of his care: "The Spirit of the Lord is on me," he said, "because he has anointed me to preach good news to the poor. He has sent me to proclaim freedom for the prisoners and recovery of sight for the blind, to release the oppressed" (Luke 4:18–19). It annoyed the Pharisees that he gathered such people as his disciples. Indeed, this was Jesus' point, that while the Pharisees had refused his offer of salvation, God had replaced them with the poor and humble. This is what Paul would later emphasize: "Brothers, think of what you were when you were called. Not many of you were wise by human standards; not many were influential; not many were of noble birth. But God chose the foolish things of the world to shame the wise; God chose the weak things of the world to shame the strong. He chose the lowly things of this world and the despised things—and the things that are not—to nullify the things that are, so that no one may boast before him" (1 Cor. 1:26–29).

Jesus put it this way, in response to another group of Pharisees who complained about the poor and sinful people he attracted, "It is not the healthy who need a doctor, but the sick. I have not come to call the righteous, but sinners to repentance" (Luke 5:31). Jesus was still talking about this on this later occasion at the Pharisee's house. In Luke 14:12–14 he said to the host, "When you give a luncheon or dinner, do not invite your friends, your brothers or relatives, or your rich neighbors; if you do, they may invite you back and so you will be repaid. But when you give a banquet, invite the poor, the crippled, the lame, the blind, and you will be blessed." That was the kind of teaching they did not like but needed to hear, just as Christians and churches need to remember that God calls us to serve others, and especially the poor and the weak and the needy. Jesus is the great example of this ministry of mercy. He later declared, "The Son of Man came to seek and to save what was lost" (Luke 19:10). That means if you are a lost and needy sinner, there is a place for you at his table.

Spurgeon, preaching on Matthew's version of this parable, in which this feast is a wedding banquet a king gave for his son, gives three reasons why God is not dishonored by the company of the poor but rather is honored in the highest. First, Spurgeon points to the gratitude of those who came from a lowly estate and from far away. The rich and powerful and self-righteous people would not have been so grateful. But, Spurgeon says, "These poor beggars picked off the streets. . . . How glad they were! One of them said to the other, 'I can hardly believe that I am really in a palace dining with a king. . . . Long live the king, say I, and blessings on the prince and his bride!' " If you realize that you are a guilty sinner, spiritually impoverished and unworthy, how grateful you will be to be brought to his banquet. In your thanks you honor God in a way the self-righteous never can.

Second, Spurgeon points out that the gathering of the poor had more joy than that of the rich. So it is for all who come to God knowing they were poor and he has made them rich, knowing they were sick and he has made them well, knowing they were blind and he has made them see, knowing they were condemned by their guilt but are pardoned by the blood of the precious Lamb of God.

Third, "the occasion became more famous than it would otherwise have been. If the feast had gone on as usual it would have been only one among many such things; but now this royal banquet was the only one of its kind, unique, unparalleled. To gather in poor men off the streets, laboring men and idle men, bad men and good men, to the wedding of the Crown Prince—this was a new thing under the sun. Everybody talked of it. There were songs made about it, and these were sung in the King's honor where none honored kings before."

More grateful, more joyful, more glorious—such is the gathering of poor hungry sinners at the banquet of the King of kings. If only we will realize that we are saved like this, that having come to God as poor and sick and dirty and blind, he yet washed us, he clothed us, he healed us and fed us and made us his own—if only we will realize that, Spurgeon concludes, "we will never leave off praising his name throughout eternity."[6]

"Christ died for the ungodly," says the Bible. "God demonstrates his own love for us in this: While we were still sinners, Christ died for us" (Rom. 5:6–8). If that is true, and Jesus' parable shows God's love for poor sinners, then none should stay away, however lowly, however poor, however guilty and sick of soul and filled with despair. None should stay away. "Go out and bring them in," says God, and Jesus went out first, coming down from heaven to purchase your seat with the blood on his cross. "Come," he now says, having flung wide the door to salvation, "Come, for everything is now ready" (Luke 14:17). And may you come through faith in him, just as you are, for truly was it said, "Blessed is the man who will eat at the feast in the kingdom of God" (Luke 14:15).

8

Three Lost Treasures

Luke 15:1–32

"My son," the father said, "you are always with me, and everything I have is yours. But we had to celebrate and be glad, because this brother of yours was dead and is alive again; he was lost and is found." (Luke 15:31–32)

The Roman philosopher Seneca was known for dining with his slaves. When confronted for this breach of social practice, he said he dined with some of them because they were worthy of his esteem, and with the rest in order to make them so. If Seneca's conduct required an explanation in Rome, you can imagine how much greater was Jesus Christ's offense for behaving similarly in first-century Judaism. Jesus' fellowship with sinners and cast-offs was a constant annoyance to the religiously correct Pharisees. Marcus Dods says, "It was a shock to the Pharisees . . . that Jesus should prefer the society of notorious sinners to their own irreproachable manners and decorous conversation. They were honestly surprised and nonplussed by His treatment of these abandoned characters. They could not understand why a teacher of holy life, instead of frowning upon the notoriously profligate, should show a preference for their society."[1]

All through our studies in the parables we have noted the importance of context to their proper understanding; usually Jesus' meaning is to be understood in terms of the question or situation at hand. That is very much the case in this chapter, where we encounter these three parables that together explain and defend Jesus' fellowship with sinners.

The Pharisees accused, "This man welcomes sinners and eats with them!" (Luke 15:2). Jesus could not have summed up his ministry more succinctly. One scholar remarks, "In the East, even today, to invite a man to a meal was an honor. It was an offer of peace, trust, brotherhood, and forgiveness; in short, sharing a table meant sharing life. . . . Jesus' meals with the publicans and sinners . . . are an expression of the mission and message of Jesus."[2] Here the most desolate and broken soul may find hope; indeed, here is the only hope any of us have: "He welcomes sinners and eats with them." And yet, lovely as this is, it was used to criticize Jesus. Then as now, the people on top loved to scorn those below. To turn their attitude upside down, Jesus gave these parables of Luke 15, which are some of his most memorable and well beloved.

Those Who Are Lost

These three parables first conspire to describe sinners as those who are lost. The first parable speaks of a sheep that has strayed from the flock. In the second, a coin has fallen off a table, rolling across the ground to a place where it cannot be seen. The third and longer parable depicts a son who has rebelled and left his father's home, likely never to be seen again. A lost sheep, a lost coin, a lost son.

Jesus describes sinners as lost, yet we cannot help but notice the three different ways in which they became lost and three different results that show the effects of sin. The sheep became lost because it was mindlessly following its appetite. This is a heedless pursuit of desires, the sheep nibbling itself off the path one mouthful at a time, out of the shepherd's sight and away from the flock. How well that describes so many people today. They begin a course of action, a style of life, not thinking of where it leads them, perhaps like the sheep never realizing the danger into which they have wandered. Sin likewise leads us into danger; the sheep is in danger for its life through predators or exposure. Thus it is for everyone, for the Bible says, "We all, like sheep, have gone astray, each of us has turned to his own way" (Isa. 53:6), a reference Jesus surely expected his hearers to recall.

In another example, a coin is lost due to circumstances that act upon it. The coin has no thought or power of its own, and likewise many become lost in sin as the result of circumstances that seem to roll them away. They enter a new setting, perhaps at work or at school, perhaps a new opportunity or a novel temptation, and they are swept into sin with no more resistance than this coin that was brushed to the floor. What is the result? They are no longer of use. Like a coin that is lost, sinners lie unused and unseen, no longer contributing the value for which they were fashioned, while God's image with which they were stamped is increasingly tarnished and covered with the dust of sinful living.

The third parable provides a portrait of our entry into sin that is more profound and more penetrating. In perhaps his best-known parable, Jesus tells of the prodigal son:

> There was a man who had two sons. The younger one said to his father, "Father, give me my share of the estate." So he divided his property between them.
>
> Not long after that, the younger son got together all he had, set off for a distant country and there squandered his wealth in wild living. (Luke 15:11–13)

Here is displayed the wicked heart of sinners, as the son spurns his father's love, misuses his gifts, and pursues the ruinous course of his depraved will. This son's request was an offense to the father's care, sin seeking as always to be its own master rather than be constrained by the bonds of goodness and loving communion with the Father. The son does not want the father, but he wants his riches—not to honor and preserve them but to consume them as fuel for his sinful passions.

Perhaps most striking is the malice the son shows to his father. Kenneth E. Bailey, writing from the perspective of the Middle Eastern culture in which these parables were given, observes how unusual it is for an estate to be divided while the father is still in good health. He points out the sharp affront implicit to this request. "Father, I cannot wait for you die," is the underlying message of this terrible demand.[3] Here, then, we have sin manifesting itself in a demand for self-rule in pursuit of wicked passions, at the cost of grave and intentional injury to the honor and love of the father. The latter, not wanting to force the devotion to which he is due, sadly honors the request.

This is not merely a picture of some people's sin, of a certain kind of sin that crops up from time to time, but this is each and every one of us in rebellion against the care and rule of God. Here is the natural person's response to God's goodness and bountiful provision, a resenting pursuit of self-will and self-rule coupled with malice to God.

Putting these three parables together, we see a comprehensive portrayal of sinners becoming lost. Some are lost because we mindlessly followed our appetites, others as we were brushed aside by circumstances. But in the third case is a more penetrating look at what underlies sin in every one of our cases. The Bible says, "The mind of sinful man is death . . . the sinful mind is enmity to God" (Rom. 8:6–7). Cornelius Van Til was once riding on a train, and across from him sat a father with a son on his lap. While the father tried to pacify the child, the little boy slapped him in the face over and over. Van Til reflected that this is sinful man in his attitude to God. Martyn Lloyd-Jones adds this:

> The terrible thing about sin is that it is rebellion against God. It is man defying God. It is man breaking God's holy law. It is man trampling upon God's sanctities. It is man setting himself up, standing up to God, and defying God. That is the essence of sin. . . . Man breaks the relationship with God and tries to set himself up as a god.[4]

This is true of the open, scandalous sinner but also of the cultured despiser of God. Make no mistake, it is this and not intellectual discovery that fuels atheistic humanism. In a telling passage, philosopher Aldous Huxley explains the source of his atheism:

> For myself, as, no doubt, for most of my contemporaries, the philosophy of meaninglessness was essentially an instrument of liberation. The liberation we desired was . . . from a certain system of morality. We objected to the morality because it interfered with our sexual freedom. . . . I had motives for not wanting the world to have a meaning; consequently I assumed that it had none, and was able without any difficulty to find satisfying reasons for this assumption.[5]

The prodigal son shows how sinful people see liberation. It is liberation to a self-governed, self-serving life that pursues its appetites and passions, no matter how wicked or how much injury and insult is done to God. People say of their indulgent sins, "No one is getting hurt," just as the prodigal must have thought as he departed from his aggrieved father. Likewise all our sins abuse the holy law of God, affront the righteous rule of God, and offend the loving heart of God. But God is not the only one hurt by our sin, for sin does not make us free but leads us condemned into bondage. Jesus put it this way: "This is the verdict: Light has come into the world, but men loved darkness instead of light because their deeds were evil" (John 3:19). He adds, "Everyone who sins is a slave to sin" (John 8:34).

Humanity's lost estate in sin is accurately described by what happened to this rebellious son. Jesus tells us that he quickly ran through his father's money, then encountered a trial in life, in this case a severe famine, which cast him into desperate need. "So he went and hired himself out to a citizen of that country, who sent him to his fields to feed pigs. He longed to fill his stomach with the pods that the pigs were eating, but no one gave him anything" (Luke 15:15–16).

Here is the bitterness of a life in sin. What a picture of spiritual depravity, this man cast off to the squalor of pigs, desperately seeking sustenance in food that is unfit for humanity. Remembering that this man is a Jew, we see here the unconscionable degradation of sin. How horrified Jesus' Pharisee hearers must have been at the thought of a Jew serving in a Gentile house tending the unclean swine and even groveling for their wretched food. Paul says, "The wages of sin is death" (Rom. 6:23); Isaiah 57:21 declares, " 'There is no peace,' says my God, 'for the wicked.' "

That is the candid bad news that Jesus sets before us, that sin leads unfailingly to this kind of condition. Yet there is also in this parable a herald of good news. Because of God's grace, rays of light still shine in this scene of darkness. In particular, these parables make three points about sinners that offer hope to the lost. First, they show that *though lost, sinners are not forgotten.* The shepherd counted his sheep and found that one was missing; the woman looked and saw that a coin of hers was lost; the father searched the horizon, longing for his son to return. So too are those whom God has chosen, whom he redeemed at the cost of his Son's precious blood, who yet have strayed away from his love. They are lost but not forgotten.

Furthermore, *they are lost yet greatly valued.* We might think that a single sheep out of a hundred is an acceptable loss, but notice that God does not reason that way. Our value is especially seen in the lost coin, for peasants had little money and such a loss was not easily made up. How much more valuable to God is the soul of a man or woman than are even this sheep and this coin to their owners.

For that reason, *sinners are lost but nonetheless are sought.* On your own your case might be hopeless; surely that is what we see with the lost sheep and the lost coin.

But God is seeking your soul, and he sent his Son into the world. Jesus said, "The Son of Man came to seek and to save what was lost" (Luke 19:10). For that reason there is hope for you. He seeks you even now, as his gospel goes forth, that you might believe and be found, that receiving him in faith you might be restored to safety, to usefulness, and to love.

For all these reasons, Jesus says in Luke 15:7, "I tell you that in the same way there will be more rejoicing in heaven over one sinner who repents than over ninety-nine righteous persons who do not need to repent." Jesus is not conceding the righteousness of the Pharisees but rather exposing how distant is their attitude from that of heaven. Shepherds value and seek sheep that are lost; a woman takes her candle and eagerly looks for the coin. How much more will God seek sinners who are lost, rejoicing when they are restored to his love.

The Path of Repentance

That is our first point, the great statement made by these parables about sinners who are lost. Second, we see especially in the parable of the lost son a vivid depiction of the sinner's repentance.

The prodigal's journey back home began "when he came to his senses" (Luke 15:17). It was his misery that aroused his sensibility: "How many of my father's hired men have food to spare, and here I am starving to death!" If that seems like a base motive, we should realize how few follow this example; indeed, it takes a mighty work of God's Spirit for us to recognize that God is the source of the blessings we have been missing. How few unbelievers recognize the squalor of their spiritual state, how close they are to the brink of ruin, how much better for them to be reconciled to God and restored to his house.

Second, notice that he made no excuses but judged himself for his sin. We see this in his planned confession, "Father, I have sinned against heaven and against you. I am no longer worthy to be called your son" (Luke 15:18–19). This is essential to any true repentance that leads to salvation; we must acknowledge and own our sin, condemning ourselves without excuse. David's psalm of repentance, Psalm 51, is a model for us in this. David says what we must say to God: "For I know my transgressions, and my sin is always before me. Against you, you only, have I sinned and done what is evil in your sight" (Ps. 51:3–4).

Third, the prodigal resolves to return to his father: "I will set out and go back to my father." Notice the humility that always marks genuine repentance: "I am no longer worthy to be called your son; make me like one of your hired men" (Luke 15:18–19). Fourth, this resolve was converted to action, as we read in Luke 15:20: "So he got up and went to his father."

Many people, I suppose, would like to repent, would like to flee their misery and go to God. But they are held back by fear of rejection, by despair for their guilt, by a despondency that says it is not worth the terrible effort. If those thoughts are holding you back, then read on to how Jesus depicts the son's return to the father: "While he was still a long way off, his father saw him and was filled with compassion for him; he ran to his son, threw his arms around him and kissed him" (Luke 15:20).

The Father's Great Love

That brings us to the third and main point of the parable of the prodigal son, which might equally be named for the prodigal father. The term *prodigal* means lavish and spendthrift, and such is the love of God portrayed in this account.

We remember it was the Pharisees' scorn over Jesus' love for sinners that prompted these parables. Here is the ultimate explanation for Jesus' ministry, namely, that God is not like the Pharisees. They looked down in scorn on those who were lost. But God is compassionate, with concern for those who suffer and grace for those who have sinned. This is the great fact that changes everything in this fallen world: God's great and boundless love that gave us his Son.

Many people wrongly think that by dying for us Jesus forced the grace of an otherwise reluctant heavenly Father. They think of God as One who is threatening, eager to condemn and to judge. If that is how you think of God, you need to realize that it was the Father who sent his Son into the world for the work of our redemption. God's great love is the motive of the gospel of grace. John 3:16 says, "For God so loved the world that he gave his one and only Son, that whoever believes in him shall not perish but have eternal life." Jesus came as our Savior with that same sacrificing love. He says, "Greater love has no one than this, that he lay down his life for his friends" (John 15:13); seeking after even one who is lost, he says, "I am the good shepherd. The good shepherd lays down his life for the sheep" (John 10:11).

Are you lost in sin, miserable in the bitterness of rebellion, but seeking a reason to return to God? Here is the reason: God's great and abounding love. Perhaps love has let you down in this life, but consider what A. W. Tozer says of God's love, a love like no other:

> Because God is self-existent, His love had no beginning; because He is eternal, His love can have

> no end; because He is infinite, it has no limit; because He is holy, it is the quintessence of all spotless purity; because He is immense, His love is an incomprehensibly vast, bottomless, shoreless sea before which we kneel in joyful silence and from which the loftiest eloquence retreats confused and abashed.[6]

That is the love revealed in the father's reaction to the sight of his son from afar. Neither the swineherd's dress nor the filth on his body nor even his wasted appearance concealed this son from these glad fatherly eyes. Jesus tells us, "While he was still a long way off, his father saw him and was filled with compassion for him; he ran to his son, threw his arms around him and kissed him" (Luke 15:20).

In most cultures, and certainly in the Middle East, it is a disgrace for a man of stature to be seen running. Men of dignity do not run; they stroll. Realize, then, that this is our Lord Jesus depicting God the Father in his indecorous love for you. Forgetting his dignity, as it were, overwhelmed by a great compassion, he runs to meet us on the way. Understand, if you are contemplating the difficult path of repentance, that God will not wait indifferently for you to perform every humble act of contrition. Seeing you from afar, reading the brokenness of your heart, he will run to meet you long before you have performed all the painful repentance you have planned.

The son tries to stammer out the speech he has prepared: "Father, I have sinned against heaven and against you. I am no longer worthy to be called your son." But the father cuts him short, not with words but with kisses. Before the son can proffer his terms of acceptance, the father's tearful embrace manifests a full reconciliation. Charles

Spurgeon preached a sermon on this, finding seven points in these mere three words: "and kissed him." The father's kisses revealed much love, much forgiveness, a full restoration, exceeding joy, overflowing comfort to the penitent son, strong assurance of salvation, and intimate communion that is the essence of restoration to God.[7] With all that awaiting the sinner who has never come to God or the Christian who has backslidden into sin, what could possibly keep you away from this overflowing love that calls to you through the gospel?

As if that were not enough, "The father said to his servants, 'Quick! Bring the best robe and put it on him. Put a ring on his finger and sandals on his feet. Bring the fattened calf and kill it. Let's have a feast and celebrate. For this son of mine was dead and is alive again; he was lost and is found.' So they began to celebrate" (Luke 15:22–24).

Here we have emblems of the sinner's return to God's favor, which together speak of bountiful blessings that flow from his love. I generally caution restraint in finding meanings for every detail in Jesus' parables, and many writers deny any specific meaning in these various articles. But, given the strong biblical background to these particular items, I find it impossible to be thus restrained in this instance.

What can the "best robe" mean to us but the imputed righteousness from God to every sinner who comes in repentance and faith, his gift that covers our sin and presents us acceptably to heaven? The robe recalls how God covered the sin of our first parents by slaying a sacrifice in their place and dressing them in its spotless innocence. Moreover, we remember the scene from Zechariah 3 that so pointedly spoke of Christ's coming work. The angel pointed to the priest covered in grime, saying, "Take off his filthy clothes." Then to the sinner he cried, "See, I have taken away your sin, and I will put rich garments on you" (Zech. 3:4). Jesus intends for each of us, as prodigal sons and daughters, to look on this scene with the joy of the prophet Isaiah, who cried, "My soul rejoices in my God. For he has clothed me with garments of salvation and arrayed me in a robe of righteousness" (Isa. 61:10).

As the robe is a symbol of righteousness, the ring "is an emblem of wealth, position, honour . . . an ornament to the hand on which it glistens. It is a sign of delegated authority and of representative character; as when Joseph was exalted to be the second man in Egypt, and Pharaoh's signet-ring was plucked off and placed upon his finger."[8] In the same way, God not only receives poor sinners but also delegates them to his work in the world as servants of the gospel.

"Put sandals on his feet," said the father, refusing the son's offer to return as a slave, for shoes were the symbol of free men. In this way the father signified the son's return to status and privilege in the house.

The fattened calf was an animal specially fed and prepared for a special occasion, and in bringing it forth for a feast the father shows two great facts of salvation. First, God reconciles sinners not only to himself but also to the community of his people, gathering many around for his second purpose, namely, a celebration of great joy. "For this son of mine was dead and is alive again," he rejoiced. "He was lost and is found.' So they began to celebrate" (Luke 15:24).

Savior of the Lost

Let me conclude with two applications, the first of which Jesus gave to the Pharisees who had accused him.

They looked down on Jesus because of the greatest, most wonderful truth about his ministry: "This man welcomes sinners and eats with them" (Luke 15:2). Similarly, many people today think Christianity should focus on condemning rather than saving the lost in the world. In response Jesus adds a third figure to this parable, namely, the elder son. He was out in the field working when a servant brought good news of his brother who had come home. Yet how different was his response from his father's:

> The older brother became angry and refused to go in. So his father went out and pleaded with him. But he answered his father, "Look! All these years I've been slaving for you and never disobeyed your orders. Yet you never gave me even a young goat so I could celebrate with my friends. But when this son of yours who has squandered your property with prostitutes comes home, you kill the fattened calf for him!" (Luke 15:28–30)

We should observe three things about this elder son. First, he stands for all those who would be saved by their works, lacking any sense of his own sin or the grace he has received in the father's love. Second, notice how out of tune is his heart compared with his father's. He does not partake of his father's love or his forgiving spirit. For all his apparent loyalty and service, he is not his father's true son; spiritually he is living in the far country among the swine. Therefore we must recognize what comes third, that he does not come into the house, where his once-lost brother went in. There is an irony here that was meant to shock Jesus' Pharisaical hearers, namely, that those who think they have earned salvation do not receive it because they refuse to enter God's feast on the basis of grace alone. Even the father's entreaties, which conclude this passage, seem not to avail. Unless the Pharisees and those like them today repent, confess their sin, rejoice over the salvation of other sinners, and enter with them by means of God's grace, there is no entry for them into the banquet of heaven.

If you want to come to Jesus Christ for salvation—and there is no other way—it must be as one who was lost but now is found. Jesus is the Savior of the lost and of them only: the lost who are sought by the Good Shepherd who died for their sins; the lost who are found by the light of God's Holy Spirit burning brightly in the hand of his lady the church, the lost who come to their senses and trusting a father's love come racing to him, finding that he is running to them in return.

That, then, is my second and closing application. Jesus "welcomes sinners and eats with them." That is the charge, and it is admitted as true. Let no sinner therefore stay away; let none stay outside God's banquet of love, either doubting his compassion or resenting his grace. This was the mark of Jesus' ministry on earth, and it still is today: Jesus welcomed sinners, and sinners welcomed him in return. He loved them, and they received his love, finding salvation for their souls and power for newness of life in him. Do not stay away; do not refuse his love. Believe in the Lord Jesus Christ, receive him who is so happy to receive you, and you will be saved.

The Shrewd Manager

Luke 16:1–13

The master commended the dishonest manager because he had acted shrewdly. For the people of this world are more shrewd in dealing with their own kind than are the people of the light. (Luke 16:8)

We are living in a time when material wealth is considered the greatest of all blessings, when money is widely acclaimed as the key to "a rich and abundant life." The cover of one of best-selling author Suze Orman's books tells us that what we need is *The Courage to Be Rich*, and that with it we will succeed in *Creating a Life of Material and Spiritual Abundance*. By tracking the titles of new spiritual trendsetters like Deepak Chopra, we find that spirituality is about

Creating Affluence, attaining *Wealth Consciousness*, and getting *What You Really, Really, Really, Really Want*.

This attitude is not restricted to the New Age aisle of the bookstore but has penetrated into the shelves somewhat generously marked "Christian." In general, as churches have become more and more worldly, many have emphasized material riches and happiness as the goal of Christianity. Especially in what is called the "faith movement," Christians are told that a lack of financial riches demonstrates a lack of faith. R. Kent Hughes cites a large charismatic church in Seattle that featured a slogan that is widely accepted today: *God Wants You to Be Rich.*[1] According to legions of heretical teachers, Christians need only to "name it and claim it," and God is sure to make them healthy and happy and rich.

But what does Jesus Christ say? That is the question Christians should most be interested in, and we should look for the answer in the Bible. Jesus' remarks on riches, it turns out, are strikingly different from what we hear today. "Woe to you who are rich," he told his disciples in Luke 6:24. In Matthew 19:24 he taught, "It is easier for a camel to go through the eye of a needle than for a rich man to enter the kingdom of God." In our passage from Luke 16 he speaks similarly, "You cannot serve both God and Money" (Luke 16:13). In Luke 9:23 he defines Christianity in terms precisely opposite of what the prosperity gospel teaches: "If anyone would come after me, he must deny himself and take up his cross daily and follow me."

The Shrewd Manager

The parable of the shrewd manager deals with spiritual resourcefulness; Jesus refers to the matter of money merely as an application of the principle he teaches here. There was a steward who managed the estate of a very rich man. Such an official had authority to conduct business on behalf of his master, making contracts and supervising their execution. This steward was accused of mismanaging the master's affairs, and he was called in to give an account. "What is this I hear about you?" the master demanded. "Give an account of your management, because you cannot be manager any longer" (Luke 16:2).

The manager seems to have had no defense, so he was sent away to clean out his desk and get his books in order and turn them in. Anyone who has faced the prospect of being fired knows something of the anguish the man must have experienced, as well as the anxiety of economic uncertainty. Jesus lets us in on the man's internal dialogue. Luke 16:3 says, "The manager said to himself, 'What shall I do now? My master is taking away my job. I'm not strong enough to dig, and I'm ashamed to beg.' " Having led a white-collar life he was no longer good for physical work, and he dreaded having to disgrace himself as a beggar. As things stood, he would have a hard time gaining employment again as a steward, and so the future looked bleak.

But the steward was a cunning man, and Luke 16:4 tells us of the solution he devised: "I know what I'll do so that, when I lose my job here, people will welcome me into their houses." Unable to save his present job, the steward made a plan that would secure the gratitude of his master's tenants, a plan he proceeded to execute flawlessly. Luke 16:5–7 tells us what he did. "He called in each one of his master's debtors," those who used his land and owed a portion of their crop to the master. The first one owed eight hundred gallons of olive oil, a massive amount that represented a great deal of money. The steward used his short-lived authority to write off half of the debt. "The manager told him, 'Take your bill, sit down quickly, and make it four hundred.'" The haste probably represents his fear of discovery and the short amount of time he had in which to pull off his scheme. A second debtor came up, owing a thousand bushels of wheat, and the steward reduced that amount to eight hundred. Scholars estimate that in both cases the savings was about 500 denarii, a single denarius representing a man's daily wage.

There are some differences of opinion regarding what is taking place in the parable. Leon Morris argues that the master had been charging a sinful and unlawfully high rate of interest and the steward made friends with the debtors by reducing the amount to a fair level.[2] The parable says nothing of this sort, however, and it is made less likely by Jesus' description of the steward as a dishonest manager. Another view, espoused by Kenneth E. Bailey, is that the manager realized from his experience that the master was a merciful man, since he did not treat him harshly when he fired the steward. Therefore his intention is to treat the debtors in a merciful manner on the master's behalf so that the master will become popular and will approve of his mercy.[3] This too fails to account for Jesus' pejorative description of the man and his actions.

The likely explanation is the most obvious one, namely, that the steward was dishonestly ingratiating himself with these debtors whose situation he improved. When he loses his job, they may offer him a place to live and perhaps a new source of income. Luke 16:4 states his intent: "When I lose my job here, people will welcome me into their houses."

So far, this is a straightforward story, but as he often did, Jesus tacked on a surprise ending in Luke 16:8, telling us what happened when the master learned of this dishonest scheme: "The master commended the dishonest manager because he had acted shrewdly."

A surprising number of scholars are thrown into confusion by this commendation, for it seems to show Jesus praising a dishonest deed. What they fail to note is that the man's dishonesty is not what is praised, but rather the resourcefulness, the cunning with which he extricated himself from a disagreeable situation. Jesus does not tell us that the master kept him on or that the unjust steward was in any way rewarded; probably he was fired and found a new home among those he helped by fleecing his master. Nonetheless his cleverness and guile were notable and received an admiring remark from the master he had cheated.

Two Ages, Two Children

Jesus' comment on this parable occurs at the end of Luke 16:8. The New International Version (NIV) reads, "For the people of this world are more shrewd in dealing with their own kind than are the people of the light." This is the point Jesus was making through this parable. Some translation issues come to bear on the interpretation of this verse. We would better translate "people of this world" as "children" or "sons of this age." Similarly "people of the light" is literally written as "children of the light." Finally, the NIV refers to children of this world being more shrewd in dealing with "their own kind," but this is better rendered as with "their own generation." Putting this together, a direct translation of this important statement would read, "For the children of this age are more shrewd in dealing with their own generation than are the children of the light."

Jesus' teaching relies on a common biblical framework

for classifying the two kinds of people in this world. People are called children of something if they belong to it or are characterized by its attributes. In John 8, for instance, Jesus called the Pharisees "children of the devil," because they served the devil's cause and acted the way the devil does. "If you were Abraham's children," Jesus argued, "then you would do the things Abraham did" (John 8:39). In like manner, Jesus states in this parable that there are children of light and by implication there are also children of the darkness, each of whom are animated by different principles and loyalties. Here the children of the darkness are identified as children of this present sinful age. By implication, the children of the light are children of a different age, namely, the one to come. Children of this age know how to get along in this present sinful world and are strongly motivated to do so, as this steward illustrates. That is what Jesus means in saying, "The children of this age are shrewd in dealing with their own generation." Alexander Maclaren explains, "A child of this world is a man whose whole thoughts, aims, and objects of life are limited and conditioned by this material present."[4]

This describes the great majority of people living today. They think little of spiritual things, and they have as their main goal and desire things that are passing with this world. As I noted, even when it comes to spiritual matters the majority of agendas today are aimed at temporal enrichment and often at the pursuit of sinful pleasures. How little thought there is of God, of judgment for sin, or of life after death. The apostle Paul speaks strikingly about children of this age, calling them "enemies of the cross of Christ." He says in Philippians 3:19, "Their destiny is destruction, their god is their stomach, and their glory is in their shame. Their mind is on earthly things."

How foolish, the Bible argues, for a man or woman created for eternity to attach his soul to things that will perish with this present age. Maclaren writes, "Fleeting wealth, fleeting honours, mortal loves, wisdom and studies that pass away with the passing away of the material. . . . these are not the things to which a man can safely lash his being, or entrust his happiness, or wisely devote his life."[5] In contrast, Paul identifies Christians by their attachment to and reliance on an age that is to come: "But our citizenship is in heaven. And we eagerly await a Savior from there, the Lord Jesus Christ, who, by the power that enables him to bring everything under his control, will transform our lowly bodies so that they will be like his glorious body" (Phil. 3:20).

Spiritual Resourcefulness

That is the way the Bible sees these two humanities, one of which aims for worldly blessing and the other for a heavenly salvation. Let us return to Luke 16:8 as I have rendered it: "The children of this age are more shrewd in dealing with their own generation than are the children of the light." The point of the parable is to show how resourceful and cunning and determined this rascal of a steward was in dealing with things of this generation or world. What is shocking, and a source of rebuke to Jesus' disciples, is that people like him show more resolve for worldly things than children of the light do for eternal things, that is, for things that belong to their generation, that age which is to come. The unjust steward showed daring, cunning, commitment, bravery, resolution—yet how seldom these things can be said of Christians in our pursuit of the things of heaven. William Hendriksen summarizes: "In worldly matters worldly people often show more astuteness or shrewdness than God's children do in matters affecting their everlasting salvation."[6]

Surely Jesus intends for us to realize that just as the worldly man had to give account of his books to his master, thus facing a temporal judgment, so too in the age to come we shall have our books brought forward for scrutiny at an eternal judgment to be rendered on our souls. The wise person, therefore, like this shrewd steward, will anticipate his or her problem and make provision for that day to come. This man was able to secure his future by making friends of the master's debtors. The only way for us to escape the judgment of God, however, is to make God our friend by the means he has stipulated in the Bible, namely, to repent of our sin, turn to Jesus Christ in faith as our Savior, and henceforth walk as his disciple in this world.

This parable differs from many of the others we have studied in that it is addressed to Jesus' disciples, as Luke 16:1 makes clear: "Jesus told his disciples." It follows on the heels of the parables on lost treasures in Luke 15, which were directed primarily to the callous Pharisees. John Calvin explains that we should understand it as a strong reproof to those who followed him:

> Christ meant . . . that heathen and worldly men are more industrious and clever in taking care of the ways and means of this fleeting world than God's children are in caring for the heavenly and eternal life, or making it their study and exercise. By this comparison He reproves our worse than spineless laziness that we do not at least have the same eye to the future that heathen men have to feathering their nests in this world.[7]

What does this tell us but that the way to be prepared, as Christians, for the eternal life to come is to emulate the worldly industry of those who seek the riches of this dying age, to practice in spiritual ways the virtues of hard work, foresight, diligence, and industry. Christians ought to be ashamed, for instance, by a comparison with a thief who breaks into houses. For a few pieces of silver and maybe a television set, he cultivates stealth, bravery, patience, and any number of other skills. Or consider the case of a young woman who longs to be a Hollywood star. She works without ceasing to enhance her beauty, she trains to sing and to act, she starves herself and exercises half to death while working for a pittance as a waitress, all for a one-in-a-million chance of attaining a fame that is fleeting at best and a fortune that will fail to give her joy in the end. Christians, by contrast, are destined to spend eternity with Christ, to reign with him, to judge the world and even angels, as Paul says in 1 Corinthians 6:1–3. If we have trusted in Christ, these things are certain, not improbable, yet we like the godless around us labor more seriously for earthly than for heavenly things, scarcely giving any thought to our spiritual improvement. How bitterly Christians complain at the slightest trials, even though we know that these light and momentary troubles are achieving for us an eternal weight of glory (2 Cor. 4:17)!

If we have anything like the shrewdness of this dishonest steward, we will instead take pains for the renewing of our minds by God's Word. We will earnestly labor to put on the new man in Christ, we will gladly take the last place knowing that it later will be first, and we will eagerly employ our temporal means to secure treasures in heaven that can never be lost. Our Lord thus calls us to examine our daily lives to see if we are showing a diligence that speaks of such wisdom, if we are making sincere effort to grow in Christ and if we are found seeking grace to conduct ourselves in a manner more consistent with our profession of faith.

Christian Stewardship

It is in light of this main point that Jesus goes on to speak of Christians and their use of money. There are three points in Luke 16:9–13, beginning with one that seems difficult to understand: "I tell you, use worldly wealth to gain friends for yourselves, so that when it is gone, you will be welcomed into eternal dwellings." This refers to the steward in the parable, who used money to make friends to provide for him after the judgment of his master. Jesus says that his disciples should use money similarly, only with an aim toward an eternal dwelling place. Some people are confused by this because it speaks of using money to make friends who will welcome us into heaven.

Let us therefore note carefully what Jesus is teaching. He says we should use money knowing that it will someday be gone. "Use worldly wealth . . . so that when it is gone," he says, referring to the fact that money can be used up and that when we die we leave it all behind. Realizing this, we should use money not just to buy perishing things but things that will last forever, to gain eternal dwellings. David Wenham explains, "The disciples are not to live for this world and its wealth, which will fail, but for the age to come, in other words for the coming kingdom of God. . . . Jesus' followers are to use their money so as to be received there."[8]

How is this done? According to Luke 16:9, we are to "use money to gain friends." It is hard to tell to whom this refers. It may point to needy persons we have helped through our gifts, who will go ahead of us into heaven and receive us there with gratitude. It may also refer to God, whom we befriend with our good and generous stewardship of the resources he gives us to use.

Does this teach that salvation is gained by works, by the wise use of money? The New Testament makes abundantly clear that we are saved by faith alone and not by works. Nonetheless true faith is always demonstrated in the way that we live. Jesus means, therefore, that those who wish to anticipate eternity in heaven and who would be shrewd and diligent in preparation for it will use their money with an eternal end in mind. Such people gladly and enthusiastically give their money for the spread of the gospel and the relief of the poor and suffering. We are saved by faith, not by money or good works; yet our use of money and our works demonstrate whether or not we have real faith and secure for us "treasure in heaven" (Matt. 19:21). Some people object, arguing that a pursuit of heavenly gain is an unworthy motive for good works. But Hebrews 11:6 assures us that believers who seek to please God do so at least partly because they "believe that he exists and that he rewards those who earnestly seek him."

Jesus' second point regarding stewardship is found in Luke 16:10–12, namely, that this present age is a time of testing that reveals our trustworthiness for greater things in the age to come. "Whoever can be trusted with very little can also be trusted with much, and whoever is dishonest with very little will also be dishonest with much. So if you have not been trustworthy in handling worldly wealth, who will trust you with true riches? And if you have not been trustworthy with someone else's property, who will give you property of your own?"

There are three contrasts here. Little is contrasted with much, worldly wealth is contrasted with true riches, which probably refers to heavenly riches, and faithfulness or honesty is contrasted with being unfaithful or dishonest. These are the terms by which our spiritual mettle is tested by our use of possessions in this life. Our money does not belong to us but to God. We are entrusted with it as stewards, and like the man in the parable we will be measured according to our use of money; like him, our books will be brought forward for an account. If we consume the wealth God has given us for our appetites, if we gather and store riches just for ourselves, neglecting so many great needs around us, we will be found unworthy of things far more significant than mere money. But if we are faithful, trusting God to provide for our needs and using our means now for the advancement of the gospel and the blessing of others, we will be trusted with far greater and with far more significant stewardships than that of mere worldly wealth. Martin Luther thus gave this wise counsel:

> Therefore we must use all these things upon earth in no other way than as a guest who travels through the land and comes to a hotel where he must lodge overnight. He takes only food and lodging from the host, and he says not that the property of the host belongs to him. Just so should we also treat our temporal possessions, as if they were not ours, and enjoy only so much of them as we need to nourish the body and then help our neighbors with the balance. Thus the life of the Christian is only a lodging for the night, since we have here no continuing city, but must journey on to heaven, where the Father is.[9]

Luke 16:13 gives the third and last application: "No servant can serve two masters. Either he will hate the one and love the other, or he will be devoted to the one and despise the other. You cannot serve both God and Money."

This reminds us that money itself is not bad, though it tempts many people to much evil. We may have and use money without folly and without sin, but only if God and not worldly wealth is our master. It is possible for a rich person to be a godly and spiritually wise Christian, exercising good stewardship of great wealth, but only if he or she has first surrendered all to Christ. It is not possible, Jesus says, to serve God and money. We will either hate the one and love the other or be devoted to the one and despise the other.

This means that if you love money, if you are determined above all else to be rich, if you find your security, like the rich fool of Luke 12, in stockpiles of cash and property and financial investments, you cannot be a Christian. You cannot be godly and cannot be saved and will not find entry into heaven. The problem is not the money but what our use of money reveals, namely, whether we are servants of God or followers of this world, whether we are children of light and of the age to come, or children of darkness and of this present passing and evil age. For those who love and serve God, money is not an evil, but its good and faithful stewardship is an eternally valuable means of worship and true spiritual service.

Who Is Wise?

This dishonest steward was commended as wise in a worldly sense, but all of us will be scrutinized for our spiritual wisdom in the things of God and of heaven (see 2 Cor.

5:10 and chapter 12 of this book). When it comes to such wisdom there are two things in view. First, we must ask what ends a person is striving toward. Are they worthwhile ends, goals worthy of our life and our heart's devotion? From the Bible's perspective, the only wise man or woman is the one who seeks to be made right with God and to gain rewards from him that last forever. No man or woman, created in God's image for eternal life, fashioned for fellowship with and service to the Lord of glory, can be called wise while aiming for the things of this passing world. "Do not store up for yourselves treasures on earth," Jesus taught, "where moth and rust destroy, and where thieves break in and steal. But store up for yourselves treasures in heaven, where moth and rust do not destroy, and where thieves do not break in and steal" (Matt. 6:19–20). Foremost among such treasures is the forgiveness of our sin and acceptance with God, great treasures that can be had without money or cost, through simple faith in Christ as the Savior of our souls.

Second, wisdom is assessed in terms of means. Are the means appropriate to the ends desired? No one can be called wise who seeks only the things of earth. But likewise, no Christian is wise who seeks heavenly treasure with worldly means, according to worldly values and principles and works. If we would be commended as wise, as this dishonest steward was in his worldly way, we must seek godly means for heavenly ends. We must, as Jesus says here, use our wealth now for things that will be of value then; knowing we cannot take it with us, we must send it ahead through its godly and generous use. If we would be wise, we will realize that our present stewardship is really a testing of our faith, proving us for greater things that are yet to come.

The shrewd steward's wisdom gained for himself a place

in the earthen homes of his master's tenants. That is about the best a child of this age can hope for. But for children of light there is so much more. The angel spoke of it to Daniel, saying, "Those who are wise will shine like the brightness of the heavens, and those who lead many to righteousness, like the stars for ever and ever" (Dan. 12:3).

The Rich Man and the Beggar

Luke 16:19–31

In hell, where he was in torment, he looked up and saw Abraham far away, with Lazarus by his side. So he called to him, "Father Abraham, have pity on me and send Lazarus to dip the tip of his finger in water and cool my tongue, because I am in agony in this fire." (Luke 16:23–24)

This next parable from Luke 16 forms part of a larger unit going back to the beginning of Luke 15. There Christ spoke of three lost treasures that were found, culminating with the famous parable of the prodigal son. The Pharisees and teachers were muttering against Jesus for eating with sinners, and he told the parables to chastise them for not rejoicing over the restoration of lost sinners to God.

This episode continues into Luke 16, Jesus warning his disciples not to become complacent because of God's grace, as we saw in our last study. Yes, God is happy to restore sinners, but that is not given as an incentive for spiritual sloth. The parable of the shrewd manager taught that Christians should be as zealous for spiritual things as worldly people are for earthly treasures.

The Pharisees overheard all this. Since they "loved money," they "sneered" at what Jesus said (Luke 16:14). Perhaps Jesus' teaching caused the people to turn and glare at them, so they felt obliged to deflect the derision. In response to their sneering, our Lord reproved the Pharisees with this next parable of the rich man and the beggar. "You are the ones who justify yourselves in the eyes of men," he said, "but God knows your hearts. What is highly valued among men is detestable in God's sight" (Luke 16:15).

A Warning to the Greedy Rich

Jesus' first point in this parable is a warning to the greedy rich. This is perhaps the most ominous of all the parables, rivaled only by the parable of the tenants, which comes later. If the parables of Luke 15 warn about a wrong attitude toward people, and if the earlier parable in Luke 16 taught about our attitude toward possessions, this parable serves as a climax dealing with both, showing God's judgment on the wicked handling of people and wealth. Jesus began:

> There was a rich man who was dressed in purple and fine linen and lived in luxury every day. At his gate was laid a beggar named Lazarus, covered with sores and longing to eat what fell from the rich

man's table. Even the dogs came and licked his sores. (Luke 16:19–21)

We have here a striking contrast. First is "a rich man who was dressed in purple and in fine linen and lived in luxury every day" (Luke 16:19). This man is not condemned for being rich, since ultimately it was God who made him rich. Among those spending eternity in heaven will be a good many people who were wealthy in this world, Abraham prominent among them. What this description condemns him for is his love of earthly riches and indifference to others in need.

First, we learn of his luxurious living. He "dressed in purple," which required a very expensive dye obtained from shellfish, so luxurious that its wear was associated with royalty. Furthermore, he wore fine linen, that is, fine-quality undergarments. William Hendriksen comments, "He was not just rich. He belonged to that class of people to whom the epithet *filthy rich* is often applied, and not without reason. His living by day in dazzling splendor marks him as a *show-off*, a strutting peacock. He wanted everyone to know that he was rich."[1]

Other indicators of his wealthy living come from the word used to speak of his gate in Luke 16:20, which suggests an opulent estate, as well as his "rich man's table," which speaks of his sumptuous culinary standards. The man employed the riches God gave him for the sake of luxury and self-glory. Compare him with Abraham, who though also rich, lived "like a stranger in a foreign country . . . looking forward to the city with foundations, whose architect and builder is God" (Heb. 11:9–10). In striking contrast to Abraham, this man's fabulous riches were all toward himself and not toward God.

Second, we see his attitude toward people in need, in Luke 16:20–21: "At his gate was laid a beggar named Lazarus, covered with sores and longing to eat what fell from the rich man's table." Whereas God's providence had made one rich, this other man was subject to suffering and humiliation. The statement that he "was laid" at the gate suggests a disability that forced him to beg.

Poor Lazarus lay in proximity to the rich man, but their lives were worlds apart. This is a contrast not at all abstract from our experience. Most of us regularly encounter such extremes of luxury and suffering, wealth and abject poverty, especially if we live in a large city. Therefore this parable lays its challenge directly before our lives. One is clothed in fabulous luxury, the other lies in rags, his body covered with sores; one dines in abundance and variety, the other starves. While the rich man struts through the world in glory, the beggar lies in disgrace, suffering the indignity described in Luke 16:21: "Even the dogs came and licked his sores."

It is inevitable that the rich man would have often passed by this wretched human being. Their eyes would have met from time to time, but the man in purple turned away, quickly passing by this unpleasant scene. Luke 16:27 reveals that he knew the poor man's name, referring to him as Lazarus, so his familiarity with the man's plight was personal. Yet he did nothing to alleviate such great suffering, despite his abundant ability to do so at slight cost to himself.

The rich man was heartless in his neglect of such great human need at his very gate. Perhaps he was orthodox in his theology; he may have dedicated a stained-glass window to his church. Yet he knew nothing of the true religion God desires, for God says, "I desire mercy, not sacrifice, and acknowledgment of God rather than burnt offerings" (Hos. 6:6).

Jesus said, "No servant can serve two masters. Either he will hate the one and love the other, or he will be devoted to the one and despise the other. You cannot serve both God and Money" (Luke 16:13). This man's handling of his wealth unfailingly revealed his true religion, and the same is true for us. Despite any claims to outward religion, his selfish use of possessions and callous disregard of his fellow man showed that he rejected God and loved money instead.

This parable is not focused on the beggar; he never acts or speaks in all these verses. All we know, other than his misery, is that his name was Lazarus. That is probably significant; the name is a variant of Eliezer, which means "God is my helper." This may indicate that in his destitution he put his faith in God, and thus we are told that when he died, "The angels carried him to Abraham's side" (Luke 16:22). That is a way of speaking about heaven that recognizes Abraham as our father in the faith. In great contrast, the rich man also died. He no doubt received a lavish funeral to which everyone came, yet he ended up in hell, "where he was in torment" (Luke 16:23).

This is Jesus' point and warning: death strips away the worldly veneer that dazzles the eyes of people, revealing only the reality as reckoned by God. All along, the poor beggar was rich toward God because of his faith, and death revealed the extent of his treasure. All along, the lavish rich man was poor in things that really mattered, and death pulled down the façade to show the real poverty of his life. J. C. Ryle observes, "Let us never give way to the common idea that men are to be valued according to their income, and that the man who has [the] most money is the one who ought to be the most highly esteemed. . . . The general teaching of Scripture is flatly opposed to it. 'Not many wise, not many mighty, not many noble are called' (1 Cor. 1:26). 'Let not the rich man glory in his riches. But let him that glorieth glory in this, that he knoweth and understandeth me' (Jer. 9:24)."[2]

A Picture of the Judgment after Death

This parable is first a warning to the greedy and callous rich, along with those who may not be rich but love money and seek after it as the object of their lives. The parable goes on to add a picture of the judgment after death, seen from the poor rich man's perspective:

> In hell, where he was in torment, he looked up and saw Abraham far away, with Lazarus by his side. So he called to him, "Father Abraham, have pity on me and send Lazarus to dip the tip of his finger in water and cool my tongue, because I am in agony in this fire."
>
> But Abraham replied, "Son, remember that in your lifetime you received your good things, while Lazarus received bad things, but now he is comforted here and you are in agony. And besides all this, between us and you a great chasm has been fixed, so that those who want to go from here to you cannot, nor can anyone cross over from there to us." (Luke 16:23–26)

This seems to picture the intermediate state after death and before the final judgment. Lazarus is said, literally, to be at Abraham's bosom, while the rich man died and went to

Hades, the holding place for the dead awaiting judgment. Scholars are nearly united in warning us not to take seriously this picture of the afterlife. This is, some say, only a stage drop or literary setting for Jesus' condemnation of greed, with no revelatory value about life after death. What is pictured here cannot be taken at face value, it is argued, because disembodied souls do not have fingers, nor can they feel bodily thirst.

A passage like this does call for caution because of its figurative representation of realities we perhaps cannot now know in any other way. Nonetheless, we remember that Jesus came to reveal truth (John 18:37), and thus we should not expect anything he teaches to be misleading. While these figures may not all have literal significance, the implications should be taken seriously. John Calvin puts it in what I think is a balanced way, writing, "The Lord is painting a picture which represents the condition of the future life in a way that we can understand. The sum of it is that believing souls when they leave the body lead a joyful and blessed life outside the world, but that for the reprobate are prepared terrifying torments which can no more be conceived by our minds than can the infinite glory of God."[3]

Our emphasis should therefore not focus on the details, such as whether or not those in hell can see and converse with saints in heaven, but rather on the spiritual implications. Jesus' point centers on the rich man's sudden realization and despair in hell. James Montgomery Boice explains, "In the moments following death, though the rich man may not have had any thoughts for heaven in this life, he now learned that there was a heaven as well as a hell and knew that he was not in heaven."[4]

There are three emphases in this picture that we should especially focus on, beginning with the final separation of the just and the damned. There were many differences between the rich man and the beggar, yet they mingled together in this life. In death, however, they are finally and utterly separated, a great chasm set between them that cannot be crossed.

This is wholly in keeping with Jesus' teaching elsewhere. In another parable, Jesus described this present life as a field in which wheat and weeds are growing together. It is only at the harvest, he said, that they are separated, the weeds tied up to be burned and the wheat gathered into the barn (Matt. 13:24–30). Later, he used yet another set of figures to speak of the final separation after death:

> All the nations will be gathered before [the Son of Man], and he will separate the people one from another as a shepherd separates the sheep from the goats. He will put the sheep on his right and the goats on his left.
>
> Then the King will say to those on his right, "Come, you who are blessed by my Father; take your inheritance, the kingdom prepared for you since the creation of the world. . . ."
>
> Then he will say to those on his left, "Depart from me, you who are cursed, into the eternal fire prepared for the devil and his angels. . . ." Then they will go away to eternal punishment, but the righteous to eternal life. (Matt. 25:32–46)

This parable of the rich man and the beggar shows the man of faith in paradise and the unbelieving sinner in the torment of hell. This separation after death is final. "Between us and you," Abraham says, "a great chasm has been fixed, so that those who want to go from here to you cannot, nor anyone cross over from there to us" (Luke 16:26). Though we are mingled together in life, in all our varied circumstances, some rich and some poor, death brings a final separation.

That leads to the second emphasis, namely, the antithesis between these two destinations, the blessing of heaven and the torment of hell. Charles Spurgeon elaborated on this:

> There are rivers of life at God's right hand—those streams can never leap in blessed cataracts to the lost. Nay, Lazarus is not permitted to dip the tip of his finger in water to administer the cooling drop to the fire-tormented tongue. . . . Heaven is rest, perfect rest—but there is no rest in hell; it is labour in the fire, but no ease, no peace, no sleep, no calm, no quiet; everlasting storm; eternal hurricane; unceasing tempest. . . . Heaven, too, is a place of joy . . . but there is no joy in hell. . . . Heaven is the place of sweet communion with God. . . . [But] there is no communion with God in hell. There are prayers, but they are unheard; there are tears, but they are unaccepted; there are cries for pity, but they are all an abomination unto the Lord. . . . It is sorrow without relief, misery without hope, and here is the pang of it—it is death without end. There is only one thing that I know of in which heaven is like hell—it is eternal. "The wrath to come, the wrath to come, the wrath to come," for ever and for ever spending itself, and yet never being spent.[5]

Many people today deny the biblical teaching of hell as eternal torment under the holy wrath of God as punishment for sin. They argue that scenes of fiery suffering are figurative. But, we ask, if that is so, of what are they a figure? Symbols are designed to correspond to the realities they portray. Jesus taught about hell extensively, often speaking of "the fires of hell" (Matt. 5:22, 30; 18:9). In Mark 9:48, he described it as a place where "their worm does not die, and the fire is not quenched," a place of outer darkness, with "weeping and gnashing of teeth" (Matt. 8:12). The Book of Revelation speaks of the devil and his minions being cast "into the lake of burning sulfur," where "they will be tormented day and night for ever and ever" (Rev. 20:10). All the dead are judged according to their deeds in this life, and "if anyone's name was not found written in the book of life, he was thrown into the lake of fire" (Rev. 20:15).

Death thus results in a permanent separation in God's judgment, with the blessed receiving eternal joy in heaven while the damned are tormented forever in hell. Lastly, this description emphasizes that these eternal destinies are determined during this life through faith in Christ on the one hand and enmity toward God and love for the world and its riches on the other.

It is popular today to speak of a second chance after death, to say that since God is so merciful he will give those who die in their sins one more opportunity when they face Jesus in the afterlife. But we see nothing of this in Scripture. Hebrews 9:27 says, "Man is destined to die once, and after that to face judgment."

Death led this beggar into eternal gain; he trusted God in his sorrows and thereby was saved. The rich man, by contrast, was condemned for his sinful love of money and neglect of his fellow man. He broke the two greatest commandments, as laid down by Jesus: "Love the Lord your

God with all your heart and with all your soul and with all your strength and with all your mind," and "Love your neighbor as yourself" (Luke 10:27). The beggar was saved by God's grace through faith; whatever sins he had were forgiven through the blood of Christ. But the unbelieving rich man, having no faith in God, was condemned by his works—his sinful deeds that wrought for him an eternity in hell. A. W. Tozer said, "There will be only one text in hell, and it may be cut against the great walls of that terrible place—'True and righteous are thy judgments, O Lord!' "[6] By that judgment this rich man found himself lost in death because of the manner of his life.

What is the point of this parable but to persuade us of the eternal significance of our present actions and attitude? Do you realize what Jesus here shows? Do you understand that your choices reveal your spiritual state—your love for God or your love for this world with its pleasures and glories and fleeting delights? You either trust God and love him—and this will be revealed by your life—or you hate God and live in enmity to him, serving instead your love of self, as shown by your avarice for possessions and disregard for others. That is the point of this parable in its portrayal of life as it leads to a destiny in death.

In death there is a chasm fixed, so that none may pass from condemnation into the courts of the just. But for all who are here living, there is yet a way in Jesus Christ. Jesus is the savior of guilty sinners, so that all who trust in him cross over into salvation. "I tell you the truth," he said, "whoever hears my word and believes him who sent me has eternal life and will not be condemned; he has crossed over from death to life" (John 5:24). Then there will be no way for the damned to come to God, but now there is a way for all who will come. "I am the way," Jesus cried, "and the truth and the life. No one comes to the Father except through me" (John 14:6). Our eternal destiny is determined in these present days of our lives—lives that may be cut short in death at any time—not only by our sins but also by whether or not we come to God by the way that is Christ, finding in him forgiveness and power to live a new life of truth and love. Thus, the Bible says, "I tell you, now is the time of God's favor, now is the day of salvation" (2 Cor. 6:2). William Arnot rightly explains,

> There is no impassable gulf now between a sinner and the Saviour; the way is open, and the perennial invitation resounds from the Gospel, "Come unto me;" but to those who pass from this life without having obeyed that call, there remaineth no more sacrifice for sin, no more a refuge from judgment.[7]

"If They Do Not Listen"

That was a lesson learned too late by the poor rich man of this parable. He was in hell, without his riches, in agony without hope. Jesus completes the scene by having him turn his thoughts to those he loved in this life, his brothers who still trod the same path that brought him to hell:

> "I beg you, father, send Lazarus to my father's house, for I have five brothers. Let him warn them, so that they will not also come to this place of torment."
>
> Abraham replied, "They have Moses and the Prophets; let them listen to them."
>
> "No, father Abraham," he said, "but if someone from the dead goes to them, they will repent."

> He said to him, "If they do not listen to Moses and the Prophets, they will not be convinced even if someone rises from the dead." (Luke 16:27–31)

This contradicts the logic so prevalent in our day, which says that signs and wonders are needed to convince people to trust in Jesus Christ. But Jesus teaches that if people will not listen to the Bible—to Moses and the Prophets, and now to the apostles as well in the New Testament—then "they will not be convinced even if someone rises from the dead" (Luke 16:31).

The lead character in Charles Dickens's *A Christmas Carol,* Ebenezer Scrooge, was much like the rich man in our parable, particularly in his lack of concern for the suffering of the poor. In that famous story, he was confronted by three visitors from the netherworld, the ghosts of Christmas past, Christmas present, and Christmas future. As a result of those visions, Scrooge's heart was pierced and he had a radical change in attitude, startling his family and acquaintances by a sudden joy and generosity. That kind of story makes good literature, but it runs directly contrary to the teaching of our Lord Jesus Christ. The problem with the rich man in this parable, as with every greedy Scrooge, is a sinful nature that in the real world cannot be so easily reformed. The problem is our hardened hearts—hardened toward God and hardened toward other people—and nothing short of the power of God is able to change our hearts.

An excellent example of this comes from just a little later in Jesus' ministry, when a visitor does appear from the dead. A friend of Jesus'—provocatively, a man also named Lazarus—died and was buried in a tomb. Jesus came and stood before the grave, crying, "Lazarus, come out!" (John 11:43). The dead man rose, came forth, and had his grave clothes removed. Yet, in response to this fantastic miracle, the Pharisees and chief priests did not take a new view of Jesus. They did not think differently about the life to come or their attitude to others. A man had come back from the dead testifying to the power of Christ for new life. And yet the incident only hardened their resolve to kill Jesus! To them it was just a threat to their power and agenda. Their hearts were not pierced by the joy Christ brought to the scene of such sadness but remained fixed in their resolve to put him to death.

How then can we be saved? It is not with signs and wonders that God presses his claims upon those living in the world but with his Word in the Bible. It is only God's Word that has the power to change the human heart from unbelief to sin, from spiritual darkness to light, from death to life. Paul therefore wrote, "I am not ashamed of the gospel, because it is the power of God for the salvation of everyone who believes" (Rom. 1:16). What we need is not a little moral persuasion but a spiritual rebirth, which comes only through God's living Word as it presses the gospel upon our hearts. As Peter wrote of believers, "You have been born again, not of perishable seed, but of imperishable, through the living and enduring word of God" (1 Peter 1:23).

Therefore do not wait for signs or miracles to break through your sin and unbelief. You must believe the gospel and be saved, for it is his Word that God has sent into the world for the salvation of all who hear and believe, repenting of their sins and flying for mercy to the cross of Christ. Ryle is right when he says:

> The principle laid down in these words is of deep importance. The Scriptures contain all that we

> need to know in order to be saved, and a messenger from the world beyond the grave could add nothing to them. . . . The dead could tell us nothing more than the Bible contains, if they rose from their graves to instruct us. After the first novelty of their testimony was worn away, we should care no more for their words than the words of any other. . . . Faith, simple faith in the Scriptures which we already possess, is the first thing needful to salvation.[8]

The stakes could not be higher. There are two destinies fixed at death, yet still open to all in this life. God has spoken grace in his gospel, and the door is open for all who will come. That is why the Bible must be our testimony in this world, the message of Christ that alone can save. The Bible and its gospel is what we must embrace and receive, learning of Christ and turning to him in faith. "Come," says Jesus, "whosoever will may come." That is what you must do—believe and call upon the Lord for salvation. Come to the Lord as a sinner needing grace, and you will be saved. Jesus said, "Ask and it will be given to you; seek and you will find; knock and the door will be opened to you" (Luke 11:9). Having saved you by faith in his cross, Christ will then open your eyes to the needy in the world around you. You will look on the poor and the lost with his eyes. He will turn your whole world upside down so that you do his will, no longer serving your selfish desires but showing mercy and love to a world that is crying in need.

The Pharisee and the Tax Collector

Luke 18:9–14

But the tax collector stood at a distance. He would not even look up to heaven, but beat his breast and said, "God, have mercy on me, a sinner." I tell you that this man, rather than the other, went home justified before God. For everyone who exalts himself will be humbled, and he who humbles himself will be exalted. (Luke 18:13–14)

Jesus' parables provide a thorough diagnosis of first-century Jewish spirituality. Most of them are told in response to a problem or sin that Jesus encountered and wanted to address. He told the parable of the good Samaritan to expose the Pharisees' lack of love toward neighbors. The parable of the rich fool typified people who think only about worldly and not spiritual treasures. The great banquet attacked spiritual presumption, and the three lost treasures of Luke 15 were spoken in response to the Pharisees' disdain for the lost whom Jesus restored. The parable of the rich man and the beggar warned the religious leaders against their love of money and neglect of the poor.

Many of the parables targeted the Pharisees, a highly respected Jewish sect who excelled in visible works and religious externals but whom Jesus accused of great spiritual corruption. Since the Pharisees represent what first-century Judaism most admired, they exemplify the spiritual state of the entire nation that first opposed and then murdered our Lord. The Judaism Jesus confronted was unloving, unmerciful, proud, and greedy for earthly riches. But above all was the sin Jesus spotlights in this parable from Luke 18, a cancer that lay at the root of all these other spiritual ailments, namely, self-righteousness.

Two Men at Prayer

Jesus' parables regularly employed irony, that is, a reversal between how things appear and how they are. This parable offers an eminent example. Jesus began, "Two men went up to the temple to pray, one a Pharisee and the other a tax collector" (Luke 18:10). The original audience expected to hear praise for the Pharisee, but Jesus exposed the Pharisee's pride and self-righteousness.

The parable probably assumes that the Pharisee attended one of the two daily periods of corporate prayer at the temple, one at 9:00 a.m. and the other at 3:00 p.m. Ordinarily the temple courts would at those times be thronged with pilgrims and other devout people who brought sacrifices and prayed aloud. Into this scene comes the Pharisee, who "stood up and prayed about himself." First, we should focus on the manner in which this religious expert came before God in prayer. Here is what Jesus tells us: "The Pharisee stood up and prayed about himself: 'God, I thank you that I am not like other men—robbers, evildoers, adulterers—or even like this tax collector. I fast twice a week and give a tenth of all I get' " (Luke 18:11–12).

There is some debate concerning the phrase "about himself." Its reference is ambiguous, referring either to the way the Pharisee stood or to the way he prayed. I think it more likely that it refers to the former, so that we would read, "The Pharisee stood apart by himself and prayed." This fits better with the impression Jesus seems to be giving, and Luke 18:13 offers a parallel when it says, "The tax collector stood at a distance." Thus the Pharisee and the tax collector stood apart from the crowd, albeit for very different reasons, the Pharisee wanting to avoid spoiling his pristine ceremonial purity through contact with lesser people and sinners.

The other rendering, that he prayed about himself, is not without support, because the Pharisee did just that. He prayed all about himself—about his attainments and superiority and deeds. He thanked God for these but seemed to think that God ought to be thanking him.

Luke introduced the parable by saying that Jesus was speaking to proud people who "looked down on everybody else" (Luke 18:9). This Pharisee is thus a glaring portrait of that kind of spiritual pride. Pride is one of the greatest and most deeply embedded sins in human nature. Jonathan Edwards wrote tellingly about it:

> Pride is the worst viper in the heart; it is the first sin that ever entered into the universe, lies lowest of all

> in the foundation of the whole building of sin, and is the most secret, deceitful, and unsearchable in its ways of working, of any lusts whatever. It is ready to mix with everything; and nothing is so hateful to God, contrary to the spirit of the gospel, or of so dangerous consequence; and there is no one sin that does so much let in the devil into the hearts of the saints, and expose them to his delusions.[1]

Saint Augustine wrote in *City of God* that pride is the calling card of the sinful City of Man. "This is," he says, "the main difference which distinguishes the two cities. . . . The humble city is the society of holy men and good angels; the proud city is the society of wicked men and evil angels. The one City began with the love of God; the other had its beginnings in the love of self."[2]

A tour through the Bible reveals how true this is. It shows us that if a person is proud, we can be sure that he or she is blind to the presence of God. When the prophet Isaiah faced a vision of the Lord in his holiness, he cried out in terms exactly opposite from this Pharisee: " 'Woe to me!' I cried. 'I am ruined!' " (Isa. 6:5). The same thing happened to Peter when on the boat he suddenly realized the deity of Jesus: "Go away from me, Lord; I am a sinful man!" (Luke 5:8). The same was true with the apostle John, who saw Jesus in his glory in the Book of Revelation and "fell at his feet as though dead" (Rev. 1:17).

All this shows that the Pharisee, for all his high reputation in religion, knew nothing of God. He stood proudly in the temple, but spiritually he was separate from and ignorant of the Lord, worshiping instead himself and all his vaunted superiority. How like so many religious people today! C. S. Lewis rightly warns us against this attitude:

> Whenever we find that our religious life is making us feel that we are good—above all, that we are better than someone else—I think we may be sure that we are being acted on, not by God, but by the devil. The real test of being in the presence of God is that you either forget about yourself altogether or see yourself as a small, dirty object.[3]

Such an example of humility is found in the tax collector, who also came to the temple to pray. Tax collectors were the scum of the Jewish world, men who collaborated with the occupying Romans and who extorted the people for their own enrichment. Darrell A. Bock says, "The two men represent polar opposites in the first-century religious culture. The Pharisee belonged to the most pious movement, while the tax collector was part of the most hated profession."[4]

They also provide polar opposites in their manner of prayer and approach to God, the Pharisee representing pride and the tax collector humility. Jesus says, "The tax collector stood at a distance. He would not even look up to heaven, but beat his breast and said, 'God, have mercy on me, a sinner' " (Luke 18:13). Like the Pharisee, he stood apart—not out of a sense of superiority but of shame. Rather than lifting his hands, he beat his breast out of grief for his sin. He spoke not of his merits but of his demerits, not bragging about what he deserved but pleading for what he did not deserve but hoped for in God's grace: "Have mercy on me, a sinner."

What are we to make of this contrast, these two approaches to God? An apparently moral and religious man coming with pride versus a criminal coming with tears and humble pleas for grace. Jesus answers, making an important statement about the religion God accepts. It was the tax collector he approved. That may have shocked his hearers, but not those familiar with the Bible. Jesus explained by quoting the Old Testament, "For everyone who exalts himself will be humbled, and he who humbles himself will be exalted" (Luke 18:13; Ps. 18:27; Prov. 3:34).

Humility is absolutely necessary to salvation, for only those conscious of their sin and need will ever come to God for grace. Indeed, it is a want of humility that keeps the great mass of people from faith and salvation. Some, like this Pharisee, for all his religion, never face the reality of their sin. Others cover their iniquity with a thin veneer of petty works and pious offerings, never seeking grace from God. The gospel of Jesus Christ demands that you confess your sin at the outset of your approach to God. This is what people hate in Christ and his gospel, and it is for rejecting this reality that many proud people will be humbled in the judgment of God. It is only those like this tax collector, conscious of their unworthiness before God, who speak the words that open the doors to heaven: "God, have mercy on me, a sinner."

A Matter of Righteousness

This parable exposes the great problem of human pride. But digging deeper, it uncovers the root from which pride grows, namely, self-righteousness. Here is the dominant theme of this parable, Luke explaining that it was spoken to "some who were confident of their own righteousness" (Luke 18:9). If pride is the poison that kills the soul, here is the cup from which it is drunk, self-righteousness.

The Pharisee's pride is revealed in the *manner* of his prayer, and his self-righteousness comes through in the *mat-*

ter or content of his prayer. He stands before God, recounting his own merits and attainments. First, he gloats about his morality, thanking God that he is better than "other men—robbers, evildoers, adulterers" and ultimately the tax collector, the very sight of whom is an offense to his eyes. Noticeably absent is any confession of his own sin or request for forgiveness—which is why he receives none from the Lord.

We should observe the method behind this madness. The Pharisee is self-righteous because his standard of comparison is other people, and especially those who stand out in depravity. He does that at which we all are so adept, finding those whose sins are obvious to us—if not to themselves—and then gloating over our apparent superiority.

But the standard for righteousness to which the Bible directs us is not that of other people but that of God. Romans 2:13 says, "It is those who obey the law who will be declared righteous." To learn God's standard, read the Ten Commandments and then Jesus' teaching on them in the Sermon on the Mount. You will find that you do not and cannot fulfill God's just demands, for the simple reason that you are a sinner. Jesus expressed God's standard, saying, "Be perfect, therefore, as your heavenly Father is perfect" (Matt. 5:48). The antidote to self-righteousness, then, is God's law, through which we are not justified but rather, as Paul writes, "we become conscious of sin" (Rom. 3:20).

The Pharisee not only justified himself by comparison to others, but also he propped up his pride on the pillar of religious works. "I fast twice a week and give a tenth of all I get," he acclaimed. The Old Testament called for one fast per year, the Day of Atonement, but the Pharisees exceeded this by fasting two days out of every seven. He also exceeded the tithing requirements, giving not merely a tenth of his income but also offering to God a tenth of all the goods he purchased. Not only had he attained moral excellence, in his view, but also he exceeded God's religious demands. Instead of looking on himself as a debtor to God, the Pharisee looked on God as a debtor to him.

In contrast is the tax collector, whose posture corresponds to the content of his prayer: "He would not even look up to heaven, but beat his breast and said, 'God, have mercy on me, a sinner' " (Luke 18:13). The difference between him and the Pharisee was not that he alone was a sinner, for the Bible says, "all have sinned and fall short of the glory of God" (Rom. 3:23). The real difference lay in their grounds of justification. The Pharisee justified himself through his comparison with others and his performance of religious externals. "Me, me, me," he boasted, pointing out how superior he was and all the things he had done. The tax collector grounded his justification in the mercy of God to which he appealed by faith. "Me," he lamented, "a sinner." Indeed, in the Greek text this comes across even stronger. "Me, *the* sinner," he cries, oblivious to anyone else and their sin but aware only of his own demerit before God. Instead of any supposed righteousness of his own, he pleads the saving grace and mercy of God.

It is these two approaches to God—as well as the two men—that Jesus has in mind when he renders his verdict. Speaking of the humble tax collector, our Lord declares, "I tell you that this man, rather than the other, went home justified before God" (Luke 18:14).

Self-righteousness is antithetical to Christianity, which relies on the grace of God alone received through faith in Christ alone. This is why there is little else more harmful to the church than when Christians fall back into self-righteousness. How common it is for Christians who were saved like this tax collector to go on to live like the Pharisee. This is what sometimes makes the church so unappealing to the world and so painful a society to its members. Such Christians thank God they are not living the sinful lives that others do, are always conscious of others' faults, trusting their effort and virtue while forgetting their sin and God's mercy. But God calls us to live in the manner we first are saved: "God have mercy on me, the sinner!" The humble manner of the tax collector is not needed merely for our entry into salvation but for the whole of our Christian lives; his plea for mercy ought to be found in all our prayers, since God's grace is the sole ground of our confidence and hope as Christians.

The Doctrine of Justification

This parable makes an important contribution to one of the chief doctrines of the Christian faith, namely, justification. Justification is so vital because it addresses the ground or basis of our standing before God. Two men in the parable are standing before the Lord—one is rejected and the other is accepted. There can be nothing more important for us to understand than the difference between the two.

John Calvin called justification "the main hinge on which religion turns."[5] The Puritan Thomas Watson wrote, "Justification is the very hinge and pillar of Christianity. An error about justification is dangerous, like a defect in a foundation."[6] J. I. Packer adds, "The doctrine of justification by faith is like Atlas: it bears a world on its shoulders, the entire evangelical knowledge of saving grace. . . . When justification falls, all true knowledge of the grace of God in human life falls with it, and then, as Luther said, the church itself falls."[7]

Justification is a legal term, speaking of the manner in which we are accepted as righteous before God. According to the Bible, justification is by grace alone. Grace is God's favor to those who deserve the opposite. God justifies or accepts us not because of our innocence or our merits. Rather, despite our guilt and demerit he justifies us by his grace. A key passage on this doctrine is found in Romans 3, where Paul writes, "All have sinned and fall short of the glory of God, and are justified freely by his grace" (Rom. 3:23–24). We can hope to be justified before God not because of what we are—for it is our sin that is the problem—but because of what God is, because he is gracious and merciful. While we deserve to be condemned, God is willing to justify us for the sake of his grace.

Justification is *by grace alone*, and it comes to sinners *through faith alone*. Paul says, "This righteousness from God comes through faith in Jesus Christ to all who believe. . . . [God] justifies those who have faith in Jesus" (Rom. 3:22, 26). Faith means believing God's Word, which is what we see in the case of the tax collector. The Bible says that all have sinned, that "there is no one righteous" (Rom. 3:10), and that is exactly how he identifies himself. "Me, a sinner," he cries. Faith requires confessing your sin and trusting God's grace, just as the penitent tax collector cries, "God, have mercy on me."

How is it, we ask, that faith allows a sinner to be declared just by a holy God? A sinner with faith is still a sinner; a believing sinner's guilt still merits God's punishment and wrath. To answer this we need a third statement about justification, namely, that justification is by grace, through faith, and *because of Christ alone*. Completing a verse I read earlier, Paul says in Romans 3:23–24, "All have sinned and fall short of the glory of God, and are justified freely by his grace through the redemption that came by Christ Jesus." Sinners are justified, says the Bible, by God's grace alone, through faith alone as that faith rests on Christ alone in his work as Savior.

The parable, however, makes no mention of Christ. As Jesus tells it, the tax collector is justified by his humility, his confession of sin and his cry for God's mercy. And yet Christ's saving work is represented by means of the word the tax collector uses for mercy. Instead of a far more common word for "have mercy," *eleison*, Jesus places a word on the tax collector's lips that specifically speaks of his atoning sacrifice on the cross. The word is *hilaskomai*, meaning "to make atonement." In its noun form, *hilastērion*, it speaks directly of the sacrifices offered daily in the temple and also of the mercy seat, where the annual sacrifice for sin was made upon the ark of the covenant.

The prayers in this parable take place in the temple, where a lamb was sacrificed twice daily. With the smoke from these burning sacrifices lingering in the air, the people came in to meet with God. The tax collector looked upon the scene with faith, whereas the Pharisee seems not to have noticed the real significance. Kenneth E. Bailey reflects on the tax collector's plea for atoning mercy and writes, "The tax collector is not offering a generalized prayer for God's mercy. He specifically yearns for the benefits of an atonement. . . . He yearns that he might stand with 'the righteous.' In deep remorse he strikes his chest and cries out in repentance and hope, 'O God! Let it be for me! Make an atonement for me, a sinner!' "[8]

This man is a known sinner, having blatantly abused God's law and harmed God's people. Yet Jesus says, "I tell you, this man went home justified before God." Though a sinner, he is justified on the basis of the sacrifice offered in his place, the atonement offered for his sins. The lambs sacrificed in the temple were but symbols of the true atonement that was yet to come. I have been quoting from Romans 3, where Paul most thoroughly discusses our justification, and the key verse there directly relates to this atonement. Paul says that justification is by grace and through faith, but on what basis? Speaking of Christ, he explains, "God presented him as a sacrifice of atonement, through faith in his blood" (Rom. 3:25).

The word rendered "sacrifice of atonement" in that verse corresponds exactly to the cry of the tax collector. He prayed, "Make an atonement for me," and God presented Jesus for just that. The word Paul uses is *hilastērion,* the name for the mercy seat on the ark of the covenant, where the sacrificial blood was spread once a year for the sins of the people. The high priest came before the throne of God, where two golden cherubim gazed down upon the broken tablets of God's law. But carrying the blood, the high priest came forward and poured it on the mercy seat, averting God's wrath, for God now saw not the broken law but the atoning blood. Paul says that Jesus Christ was that sacrifice, his the blood that takes away our sin. The tax collector cried, "O God, make an atonement for me, a sinner!" and at the cross God presented his own Son for just that. The tax collector, therefore, was justified by God's grace, through his faith in the atonement God offered in the precious blood of Christ.

It is on this basis alone that God receives any sinner's prayer. But more importantly, it is only on this basis that God receives any sinner himself or herself, forgiving our sins and clothing us with the righteousness of Christ. Two men stood before the burning sacrifice, one with faith in his works and the other trusting only in the blood that was shed for sinners. Jesus died for sinners. But only those who renounce their works, confess their sins, and trust in him alone, his shed blood for their redemption, are justified before God's holy throne.

Gospel Math

This is the Christian gospel, that Jesus died for sinners that they might be justified through faith in his blood. This is the best of good news for every broken sinner seeking grace in the mercy of God. But it is bad news for all who claim a righteousness of their own. It is bad news to those like this Pharisee, proudly denying that they have sinned, not realizing what Jesus says, that "everyone who exalts himself will be humbled, and he who humbles himself will be exalted" (Luke 18:14).

The doctrine of justification is especially associated with the apostle Paul, whose writings most clearly set it forth. But this teaching is found all through the Bible—it is first portrayed outside the gates of Eden when God clothed our first sinful parents in the skins of innocent substitutes who were slain—and here it comes to us from the lips of our Lord. And yet there is good reason why Paul loved this doctrine and placed so much weight upon it.

We remember how close was Paul's relationship to Luke, the writer of this Gospel, and thus Paul must have known about this parable. Paul would have listened to it as his own story, one that he tells in theological terms in Philippians 3. There he reminds us that he was a Pharisee and that his attitude was the same as that of the proud man in this parable. He writes of all his former self-righteousness, based on a surface observance of the law, all of which he describes as "confidence in the flesh": he was "circumcised on the eighth day, of the people of Israel, of the tribe of Benjamin, a Hebrew of Hebrews; in regard to the law, a Pharisee; as for zeal, persecuting the church; as for legalistic righteousness, faultless" (Phil. 3:5–6).

These were Paul's spiritual assets before he came to know Jesus Christ. He, like the Pharisee in this parable, stood before God talking about himself—about what a good person he was, about all he had done, just as people insist today, "I'm a pretty good person." Paul thought he was a very good person, and with his assets he looked down on the common sinful rabble and boldly stood before God on his merits.

Seeing Jesus changed all this. In Jesus, Paul gained a new standard for comparison, and there he saw what a sinner he really was. He found in Christ's gospel a different way to be justified before God, a way that was offered to sinners like him. Realizing this, he writes, "Whatever was to my profit I now consider loss for the sake of Christ." No longer trusting in his works, in his pedigree, in all his religious performance, he says, "I consider them rubbish, that I may gain Christ and be found in him, not having a righteousness of my own that comes from the law, but that which is through faith in Christ—the righteousness that comes from God and is by faith" (Phil. 3:8–9).

Paul learned what Jesus teaches in this parable, that all our self-righteous merits are not assets but liabilities. Even our best works are corrupted by sin and are unable to conceal our guilt. Worse, they keep us from the only Savior, whose perfect righteousness God offers to us as a gift. Paul therefore removes all his former assets, leaving nothing of his own, and taking hold of Christ in their place. He says what we sing in the hymn "Rock of Ages": "Nothing in my hands I bring, simply to the cross I cling. Naked come to thee for dress, helpless look to thee for grace. Foul, I to the fountain fly; wash me Savior, or I die." Paul's desire is the only one that brings salvation to sinners: "That I may gain Christ and be found in him, not having a righteousness of my own that comes from the law, but that which is through faith in Christ." That is how he reckoned himself before God through faith alone, and it is the only mathematics that leads to salvation.

How do you add things up? How do you stand before God? Do you come in your own supposed righteousness, perhaps admitting a little need for grace and help but standing before God like this Pharisee? Jesus says you will never be justified that way, you will never be saved, you will never get to heaven, because admit it or not you are a sinner and the holy God will reject you.

Or are you like this tax collector, so conscious of your sin that you barely think to come to God, finding it hard even to walk in the doors of a church? If you will look in faith to the shed blood of the sacrifice God has made, the Lamb of God Jesus Christ, God will receive you with gladness. If you come in the way God has provided, he will make you his beloved child, and he will call you and lead you into a new and holy life. If you come to God as a sinner seeking grace through the saving work of Christ alone, begging for God's mercy in the atonement he has offered through his Son, then Jesus says of you, "I tell you, this one is justified before God."

12

The Returning King

Luke 19:11–27

A man of noble birth went to a distant country to have himself appointed king and then to return. So he called ten of his servants and gave them ten minas. "Put this money to work," he said, "until I come back." (Luke 19:12–13)

The parable before us could hardly have been given in a more dramatic setting. Jesus was traveling through Jericho and had just invited himself to dine with the chief tax collector of that place, a notorious sinner named Zacchaeus. The crowd was alarmed, but before their eyes Zacchaeus repented of his sins and offered to make full restitution for all the harm he had done. Jesus explained the encounter, saying, "The Son of Man came to seek and to save what was lost" (Luke 19:10). Our next parable begins in this context. Luke writes, "While they were listening to this, [Jesus] went on to tell them a parable" (Luke 19:11).

This passage brings to a conclusion a major unit of Luke's Gospel, known as the Travel Narrative, which started in Luke 9. There occurs Peter's great confession of faith in Christ, followed by the transfiguration, when our Lord appeared to three of his disciples in glory. This is a main turning point in Luke's Gospel as it was in the ministry of our Lord. Immediately afterward Jesus declared the mission of his cross, to which he then started to advance. Luke records this new beginning in Luke 9:51: "As the time approached for him to be taken up to heaven, Jesus resolutely set out for Jerusalem." The Travel Narrative that follows, in which almost all the parables we have studied are found, recounts that journey until his arrival at Jerusalem on Palm Sunday. The parable of the returning king comes at the end of that journey; immediately after it comes Jesus' triumphal entry into Jerusalem. The significance of the parable is therefore highlighted by the important crossroads it occupies in Jesus' ministry and life.

Delay of the Kingdom

Luke sets the occasion by telling us that Jesus "was near Jerusalem and the people thought that the kingdom of God was going to appear at once" (Luke 19:11). Drawing near to the holy city after so eventful a journey undoubtedly heightened the disciples' expectation. A number of recent events would have especially focused their minds on the idea of Jesus' coming kingdom. As he entered Jericho that day a large crowd gathered along the road. Included was a blind beggar who cried out, "Son of David, have mercy on me" (Luke 18:39). When Jesus healed the man, the whole crowd marveled, and thoughts of an imminent messianic kingdom filled the air. Norval Geldenhuys writes, "There is probably among many of the multitude an expectation that the sovereign dominion of God will now, through Him as the Messiah, be speedily and miraculously revealed."[1]

Jesus was on the threshold of an epochal turning point, only not the one the crowds and even his disciples so keenly anticipated. Soon he would ride into Jerusalem to fulfill a long-standing hope for a king. Yet it was not to assume earthly power that he came. As Jesus spoke this parable, he was only a week away from his gruesome death on a cross, rejected by the Jews and brutalized by the Romans. At his trial, the question of his kingship would arise; "My kingdom is not of this world" (John 18:36) would be his reply. Pilate would respond by attaching a sign, prophetic and ominous, to the cross: "This is the king of the Jews" (Luke 23:38). Jesus was a king, the true King, but one who was hated by his wicked subjects and murdered by the powers of this world. It was in anticipation of these events that Jesus told this important parable.

The parable begins, "A man of noble birth went to a distant country to have himself appointed king and then to return" (Luke 19:12). This scenario was familiar to Jesus' hearers, for their rulers traveled to Rome to receive their kingship from the emperor. A famous example was that of Archelaus, who went there seeking his crown after the death of his father, Herod the Great, in 4 B.C. This was a famous incident because a delegation of Jews also went to Rome to protest his enthronement. Archelaus was cruel and generally unfit to rule, and so the people pleaded before Augustus Caesar with words like those Jesus uses in Luke 19:14, "We don't want this man to be our king." It happens that Archelaus's palace was built in Jericho, so Jesus may have preached this sermon in its shadow. The connection, therefore, is unmistakable. It is astonishing that our Lord should compare himself with so loathsome a figure as Archelaus, and yet it served the narrow purpose of his teaching. As in that famous example, he would travel to a distant land—not Rome, but heaven—to receive his crown, then to return and establish his reign.

These opening verses give us vital information for a Christian view of history and of our Lord's reign as king. The Bible says that Jesus came to earth with a right to rule but instead allowed himself to be crucified for our sins. God therefore raised him from the grave and elevated him to his right hand in the heavens, where Jesus received the heavenly kingdom. Even now, he reigns in heaven as our king. The remaining purpose of history is for the ingathering of his kingdom people through faith in the gospel, after which he will return to end that history with the final judgment and the beginning of his eternal reign. Christians are citizens of the heavenly kingdom that will one day be universal, awaiting with our Lord its manifestation in the time of his return. Our anticipation fills our hymns as we look forward to that day: "The head that once was crowned with thorns is crowned with glory now; a royal diadem adorns the mighty Victor's brow . . . Thou art coming, O my Savior, thou art coming, O my King . . . well may we rejoice and sing."

A Charge to Christ's Servants

That view of history and our relationship to Christ has the most profound impact on our view of this present life. We see this in Luke 19:13, where Jesus tells of the nobleman's dealings with his servants prior to his departure: "He called ten of his servants and gave them ten minas. 'Put this money to work,' he said, 'until I come back.' "

A mina was an amount of money that amounted to one hundred denarii, about three and a half months' wages. The nobleman entrusted this amount to each of his ten servants, charging them to employ it to his profit while he was gone.

This is one of the points of difference between this parable and a similar one told in Matthew 25. There Jesus gave different amounts to different servants, "each according to his ability" (Matt. 25:15). Here the servants are each given the same amount. This detail has caused many expositors to teach that Matthew's version emphasizes the variety of gifts and ability that Christ bestows upon his people. Luke's Gospel, in contrast, speaks of the one resource we all have equally and in common, namely, the gospel message. This seems to fit the fact that, in contrast to Matthew's parable, Luke's nobleman gives a comparatively small amount of money, just as the gospel is of apparently little value in the coin of this world.

The gospel is the great resource of all who serve the Lord in this present age; it is God's power for the salvation of those who believe (Rom. 1:16). We are charged to diligently employ the gospel, together as a church and individually in our various relationships and roles. "Put this to work," says our Lord, even as he said in the Great Commission, "Go and make disciples of all nations" (Matt. 28:19).

So mighty is the gospel that all we have to do is display it, in our lives and in our testimony, and God's Spirit works a harvest for our Lord. This, perhaps, is reflected in the words of the first servant, in Luke 19:16, which indicates that the resource Christ gives has its own power to grow. When asked how he did, he told the Lord, "Sir, your mina has earned ten more." In the same way, it is not we who give the Lord increase, but his Word as empowered by the Spirit. Ours is to invest and diligently employ the gospel, confident that God will provide the power for its success. This is consistent with how Paul explained the ministry in Corinth: "I planted the seed, Apollos watered it, but God made it grow" (1 Cor. 3:6).

Jesus does not specifically identify the minas with the gospel, and we probably should take them as all the resources he provides us. Chief among them is the gospel, but included are gifts, talents, money, time, positions, relationships, and so on. The charge is to employ our lives profitably for him with all the resources he gives. Christians in this world are Christ's servants and are to be busy about his work, serving his interests and advancing his kingdom as we await his return.

The implications of this parable are as practical as they are radical. We are not to live for ourselves, for our pleasure and much less for sin! The mina Christ gives us is not to be spent on ourselves, on our temporal or spiritual comfort, but to be put to work on his behalf. If you know and understand the gospel and the doctrines of the Bible, these are not just for your benefit but that you might act upon them and especially proclaim and explain them to others. So also with our material resources. We are to give physical and emotional and spiritual help to a needy world around us, and especially to fellow citizens of Christ's kingdom. In doing so we serve our king who now is and is yet to come. As Matthew 25:40 tells us, when he returns he will reward us, saying, "I tell you the truth, whatever you did for one of the least of these brothers of mine, you did for me."

The King's Accounting

The nobleman crowned king in due time returned to his subjects, with words that clearly relate to our Lord Jesus' future return to earth in glory and power. "He was made king . . . and returned home. Then he sent for his servants to whom he had given the money, in order to find out what they had gained with it" (Luke 19:15).

The first two servants gave a favorable report and were abundantly rewarded. "The first one came and said, 'Sir, your mina has earned ten more.' 'Well done, my good servant!' his master replied. 'Because you have been trustworthy in a very small matter, take charge of ten cities.' The second came and said, 'Sir, your mina has earned five more.' His master answered, 'You take charge of five cities'" (Luke 19:16–19).

Notice, first, that when Jesus returns and calls his servants to account, a good report is one that speaks of increase to his kingdom. One servant had earned a tenfold profit and the other a fivefold profit, and they both received the Lord's approval. Second, we observe the disproportion between what the servants earned for the king and the reward the king gave them. For earning ten minas the first servant was given charge of ten cities, a colossal reward that shows Christ's grace in dealing with his own. The Bible says that God will judge the church, but look at this judgment! The reward is out of all proportion to what has been accomplished. The king was not bound to give any reward; all that they had was from him and for him. Yet his judgment overflows with superabounding grace!

Third, we see that there is a comparative relationship between what the servants earned and what they received. The one who gained a tenfold increase is rewarded with ten cities; the one who gained fivefold received five cities. Jesus explains the principle guiding this dispersal, as Matthew 25:21 puts it: "You have been faithful with a few things; I will put you in charge of many things."

This tells us something of our Lord's method in giving us work for this present life. Yes, he seeks to gain a profit for his kingdom. But just as importantly, he is testing and training us for greater usefulness in the age to come. Charles Spurgeon explains, "This nobleman said to himself, 'When I am a king I must have faithful servants in power around me. My going away gives me an opportunity of seeing what my servants are made of. I shall thus test their capacity and their industry, their honesty and their zeal. If they prove faithful over a few things they will be fit to be trusted with greater matters.'"[2]

That puts a different light on the seemingly small responsibilities the Lord gives us now. So many of us think there is little import to the way we live, our use of money and time and abilities, our participation in the church and witness to the world. But this parable makes plain that there is a direct relationship between our present fidelity and diligence and our future scope for service to the Lord. Hudson Taylor put it best, saying, "A little thing is a little thing, but faithfulness in a little thing is a big thing." Our faithfulness is a big thing because it matters to Christ and expresses our devotion to him. It is also preparation and a test for service in the day of our Lord's return.

Questions about Rewards

This teaching will raise some questions that I want to handle directly. First, does this mean there will be rewards for Christians in heaven? The answer clearly is yes. The whole point of this parable is that there is a relationship between our faithfulness now and rewards we will receive in the life to come. People tend to think of such rewards in terms of earthly riches—money, possessions, good seats. But

Jesus expresses it in this parable in terms of increased opportunity to serve him. As Joachim Jeremias puts it, "The reward of a duty done is a duty to be done."[3] Christ's faithful servants will be viceroys with him in his eternal reign; our reward is companionship with him and fellowship in the blessed employment of glory. Thus he spoke to his disciples, "At the renewal of all things, when the Son of Man sits on his glorious throne, you who have followed me will also sit on twelve thrones, judging the twelve tribes of Israel" (Matt. 19:28).

This leads to another question. Does this mean that some will have more rewards or a higher place in heaven than others? The answer is yes. One receives ten cities and another five. Paul asserted the principle in 1 Corinthians 3:8, "Each will be rewarded according to his own labor." Matthew Henry explains it this way: "This intimates that there are degrees of glory in heaven; every vessel will be alike *full*, but not alike *large*. And the degrees of glory there will be according to the degrees of usefulness here."[4] This does not mean that prominent Christians in this life will necessarily be the greatest in heaven. Indeed, there will no doubt be a great many surprises in that regard. When his disciples were found jockeying for position in the age to come, Jesus asserted the priority of humble servanthood: "If anyone wants to be first, he must be the very last, and the servant of all" (Mark 9:35). On this basis, therefore, we should not be surprised to learn that in many cases the church's janitor will find more honor in heaven than the pastor does.

This leads to another question, even an objection: Does not this violate the idea of salvation by grace through faith, apart from works? The answer is no. Sinners are forgiven, clothed in Christ's righteousness, and accepted by God as beloved children by grace alone and through faith in Christ alone. None of our works, tainted as they are by sin, can bring us over from death into life. But having saved us by grace, God treats us as a father does his children, including the use of tests and rewards. Yet, we ask, how can we get rewards for what is after all God's work of grace in us? Everything good we do is the result of God's grace and is to his glory, so how can we be rewarded for them? The answer is by God's grace in Christ. It is in Christ that our works are received by God with favor and rewarded by his grace. The Westminster Confession of Faith puts it well, remarking that just as believers are accepted in Christ, so also are the believer's works accepted in Christ. God "looking upon them in His Son, is pleased to accept and reward that which is sincere, although accompanied with many weaknesses and imperfections" (16.6).

Does this mean, then, we should be motivated to serve Christ by a desire for rewards in the age to come? Is this an appropriate motive for Christians? Aren't we supposed to be self-sacrificing, not self-serving, in our faith? The biblical answer is that yes, we are to be motivated by an awareness of future reward in Christ's return. This, after all, is why Jesus told this parable, to motivate faithful service while he is away. Paul writes, "We must all appear before the judgment seat of Christ, that each one may receive what is due him for the things done while in the body, whether good or bad" (2 Cor. 5:10). He is speaking of a valid Christian motive when he adds, "So we make it our goal to please him" (2 Cor. 5:9).

True Christians cannot be condemned for sin, for as Romans 8:1 says, "There is now no condemnation for those who are in Christ Jesus." In Romans 8:31–34, Paul reasons that God will justify those who trust in Jesus, who gave his blood for our salvation. Nonetheless, as Jesus makes clear in this parable, he will call us to give an account of our lives. First Corinthians 3:12–15 explains that our "work will be shown for what it is. . . . It will be revealed with fire, and the fire will test the quality of each man's work. If what he has built survives, he will receive his reward. If it is burned up, he will suffer loss; he himself will be saved, but only as one escaping through the flames." Jesus exhorted in the Sermon on the Mount, "Store up for yourselves treasures in heaven, where moth and rust do not destroy, and where thieves do not break in and steal" (Matt. 6:20). These statements all serve to motivate us to a wise use of our lives for heavenly reward.

With that having been observed, the Christian does not look upon rewards as the primary motive for godly works. Our main motive for sharing the gospel with the world is a sincere compassion for the lost and a genuine zeal for Christ's kingdom. What leads a Christian away from sin and into new paths of righteousness is a longing to please our loving Lord and Savior, to know his joy in our obedience. Yes, we are to realize what our Lord is teaching and take a sober account of our lives, to thus apply ourselves seriously, and to seek many crowns to lay at Jesus' blessed feet on the day of his return. But our main joy is the increase of his glory and the knowledge of his pleasure in our love for him. All the while, especially in times of hardship or doubt, God's people are heartened by an awareness of what John Newton in "Glorious Things of Thee Are Spoken" describes as "solid joys and lasting pleasures" that await us in heaven and that "only Zion's children know." It is this perspective that enabled the apostle Paul to tells us that "our light and momentary troubles are achieving for us an eternal glory that far outweighs them all" (2 Cor. 4:17).

The Sword of Judgment

Jesus goes on to speak of another servant who gives a very different report. "Then another servant came and said, 'Sir, here is your mina; I have kept it laid away in a piece of cloth' " (Luke 19:20). Here is one who has not labored for the king, has not borne fruit, has not earned profits while the master was away. For him, Jesus has no approval but only condemnation.

This servant had an excuse: "I was afraid of you, because you are a hard man. You take out what you did not put in and reap what you did not sow." The king's reply is startling: "I will judge you by your own words, you wicked servant! You knew, did you, that I am a hard man, taking out what I did not put in, and reaping what I did not sow? Why then didn't you put my money on deposit, so that when I came back, I could have collected it with interest?" (Luke 19:21–23).

The king is not affirming the wicked servant's opinion of him but rather judges him according to the servant's words. If the thought of reward failed to motivate him, the fear of retribution should have! The faithless servant's words show that he does not even know his master, for his description is contrary to the grace we saw in the previous examples. Furthermore, he does not love him, for he was unwilling to put forth effort if it was only for the master's benefit. You see why Jesus calls him "you wicked servant!"

There is some question as to whether this third servant represents fruitless Christians who are barely saved, like Paul's man saved as through a burning house (1 Cor. 3:15). I think it is better to understand this man as rejected by the king and therefore condemned to judgment. Matthew's similar parable, which is very close in this detail, says of the man, "Throw that worthless servant outside, into the darkness, where there will be weeping and gnashing of teeth" (Matt. 25:30). The faithless servant thus stands for professing Christians who are revealed as unbelievers by their lack of fruit. The king says to those standing by, "Take his mina away from him and give it to the one who has ten minas" (Luke 19:24). When they object, he replies, "I tell you that to everyone who has, more will be given, but as for the one who has nothing, even what he has will be taken away" (Luke 19:26). Those who earn profit for the Lord are thus abundantly rewarded with future responsibility and opportunities to bear fruit.

The king has been dealing with his servants, but now he addresses those who had openly rebelled against his reign. "Those enemies of mine who did not want me to be king over them—bring them here and kill them in front of me" (Luke 19:27). That is how kings respond to traitors, and in light of what was about to happen to Jesus, these words were stark indeed. Luke 19:14 depicts what took place just a few days later, when in hatred of Jesus a delegation of Jews went to Pilate saying, in effect, "We don't want this man to be our king." John 19:15 records the dreadful words they spoke: "We have no king but Caesar," cried the chief priests, men supposedly devoted to God. "Let his blood be on us and on our children!" called out the people (Matt. 27:25).

This parable foretells in stark terms God's judgment on such rebels, and it applies equally to those today who reject Christ's rule as king. People don't like to accept such teaching, but the Bible clearly speaks of the wrath of Christ when, as Paul writes, "The Lord Jesus is revealed from heaven in blazing fire with his powerful angels. He will punish those who do not know God and do not obey the gospel of our Lord Jesus. They will be punished with everlasting destruction and shut out from the presence of the Lord" (2 Thess. 1:7–9). It is easy to oppose and mock Jesus now, while he is away, and many reject him, saying, "We don't want this Jesus to be our king!" Is that what you say? Do you reject Jesus' rule over your life? Understand, then, that your opposition will not produce his downfall, will not deny him the crown, but will only bring the sword of his fury on the great day of his coming. In "Day of Judgment! Day of Wonders!" John Newton writes,

> Day of judgment! Day of wonders!
> Hark! the trumpet's awful sound,
> Louder than a thousand thunders,
> Shakes the vast creation round.
> How the summons will the sinner's heart
> confound!
>
> But to those who have confessed,
> Loved and served the Lord below,
> He will say, "Come near, ye blessed,
> See the kingdom I bestow;
> You forever shall my love and glory know.

The Threshold of Eternity

Jesus stood along the road in Jericho, a single day's march from his final earthly destination, the place of his rejection and crucifixion. If ever a lord had the right to place duties on his servants it was Jesus, who was about to pay so high a price to redeem us from our sins. Here he charges all his disciples to profitably engage in service of his kingdom in this time of his delay, some with one gift and some with another, all of us with the gospel message he has given us to share. When he returns in his kingdom, he will ask each to account for what he has done, rewarding his faithful servants with superabounding grace, casting out all who have falsely professed him, and destroying in his wrath all who hated him and opposed his reign in this world.

Do you understand what this means for these present years of your life? To the person without Christ, this life is all there is. Death is the end, and all reward is here in this life. No wonder such a person thinks the way Paul put it: "If the dead are not raised, 'Let us eat and drink, for tomorrow we die'" (1 Cor. 15:32). But Christians know that we live now on the threshold of eternity. A great and glorious future awaits us in the resurrection age to come. We stand at the edge of the old world, gazing upon a new and eternal creation suffused with the glory of God. This present life is, for us, but a prelude to glory, a preparation and a foretaste of the heaven ahead.

We look forward to that future, yet these alone are the years of our faith, the time of testing and preparation for all that will come. How powerfully this speaks of the eternal significance of our present actions! We now are like Israel sojourning through the desert with Canaan just ahead. And just as faithful Caleb, who alone with Joshua obeyed and served the Lord, was rewarded with grand estates in the Promised Land, so we too may gain cities in the day of our king's coming, through the faithful employment of the gospel in this age, along with every resource the Lord puts at our disposal. Therefore, while the short years of this present life are the most trying we shall ever know, in this sense they are also the most significant in all eternity, for on the anvil of our present lives eternal destinies and rewards are being forged.

The apostle John comforts us in his first epistle, writing that through faith in Christ we are now the children of God. He says that while we do not understand what awaits us in heaven, we do know this: "We know that when he appears, we shall be like him, for we shall see him as he is." With that in mind, he concludes, "Everyone who has this hope in him purifies himself, just as he is pure" (1 John 3:2–3). Paul candidly reminds the Corinthians that Christ will call his servants to account when he comes. So, he says, "We make it our goal to please him" (2 Cor. 5:9). Perhaps most inspiring, the angel reminded Daniel in his days of dark trial, "Those who are wise will shine like the brightness of the heavens, and those who lead many to righteousness, like the stars for ever and ever" (Dan. 12:3). May each of us take these things to heart, not growing faint in our difficulties but pressing on to receive an eternal reward through Jesus Christ, our Savior and returning King.

13

The Wicked Tenants

Luke 20:9–19

Then the owner of the vineyard said, "What shall I do? I will send my son, whom I love; perhaps they will respect him." But when the tenants saw him, they talked the matter over. "This is the heir," they said. "Let's kill him, and the inheritance will be ours." So they threw him out of the vineyard and killed him. (Luke 20:13–15)

We conclude our studies in Jesus' parables with one that contains many of the themes we have earlier considered. Jesus' parables speak strongly against the Pharisaical establishment, and this parable denounces the leaders in a most blatant manner. Furthermore, this parable sheds light on the delay of Jesus' kingdom, as well as his rejection and death. Just like other parables, this one calls for a radical commitment to Jesus and a choice that determines our eternal destiny. When Jesus comes into our lives, he comes to make a whole transformation, to turn our lives upside down. In this parable is the heart of his message, that he comes from God to claim our allegiance and service, to turn rebel sinners back to God, to turn our lives from self-centered sin to a God-centered salvation.

The drama is heightened by the setting in which Jesus speaks, at the brink of his arrest and crucifixion. Here is Israel's last chance to repent and believe. Here too is a call for us to repent and return to God for forgiveness and newness of life.

The Wicked Tenants

Luke 20 begins by telling us that Jesus was "teaching the people in the temple courts and preaching the gospel." The religious leaders confronted him there, demanding, "Tell us by what authority you are doing these things. Who gave you this authority?" (Luke 20:1–2). Jesus, knowing their false motives, refused to answer directly, instead telling this parable that gave his answer clearly enough.

He began, "A man planted a vineyard, rented it to some farmers and went away for a long time" (Luke 20:9). Jesus' hearers would undoubtedly have connected this vineyard with Israel. Many Old Testament texts make this connection (see Isa. 5:1–7; Ps. 80:8–15). Furthermore, the temple building, where Jesus was teaching, was adorned with a richly carved grapevine, to which wealthy Jews contributed jewel-encrusted grapes and leaves. The vineyard was a symbol of Israel sacred in the hearts of the people.

Jesus points out that this vineyard belonged not to the tenants but to the owner who planted it. This owner is God, and from this perspective we see that the vineyard is not merely Israel as such, but rather the place of privilege and blessing that Israel had long enjoyed as God's people. The Jews, and especially their leaders, are depicted as having been put in charge of God's vineyard to bear a harvest of fruit for him. "At harvest time," Jesus continued, "he sent a servant to the tenants so that they would give him some of the fruit of the vineyard" (Luke 20:10). As Jesus has frequently asserted in his parables, God demands fruit from his people. But Israel resented God's demands and denied him what he sought. When a servant sent by the owner arrived, "The tenants beat him and sent him away empty-handed" (Luke 20:10).

This is, in fact, Israel's history. God saved Israel from the bondage in Egypt, planting the nation in the Promised Land like a choice vineyard, seeking the good fruit of faithful worship and holy lives. But Israel continually disobeyed God and engaged in the worst sorts of idolatries. Generation after generation saw faithless leaders and false prophets who led the people astray. God therefore sent his true prophets to call them to repentance and faith. These were despised by the people and persecuted by the leaders.

The Old Testament bears abundant testimony to this rendition of Israel's history. Elijah, one of the earlier prophets, was driven into the wilderness and constantly harassed. According to tradition, Isaiah was sawn in half. Jeremiah was arrested and tossed into a muddy cistern to die. Zechariah was stoned to death within the temple. An example recent to Jesus' audience was that of John the Baptist, who was beheaded by King Herod as the reward for his faithful witness. No wonder Jesus lamented, "O Jerusalem, Jerusalem, you who kill the prophets and stone those sent to you, how often I have longed to gather your children together, as a hen gathers her chicks under her wings, but you were not willing!" (Luke 13:34).

Jesus' telling of this history reveals the wonderful patience of God, his gracious forbearance toward the sin of his people. God had every right to respond to sin with immediate judgment, yet again and again he came to them, sending servant after servant to call them to repent. With pity he looked on those who harmed him. With love he pursued those who had fled, redeeming many who were lost. This is what God is like even today, abounding in mercy and grace. Charles Spurgeon wrote, "If you reject him, he answers you with tears; if you wound him, he bleeds out cleansing fluid; if you kill him, he dies to redeem; if you bury him, he rises again to bring resurrection."[1] Truly, who is like our God, and what a tragedy that so few accept his offer of salvation!

But the parable presents the vineyard owner with a problem. He sent a servant who was rejected. Another was sent, and "they beat and treated him shamefully." Yet another "they wounded . . . and threw out" (Luke 20:11–12). Things were getting worse and not better. The owner's profits were still denied, and the tenants were growing more unruly and hardened against his claims.

This seems to be quite a quandary. The owner wanted a harvest; that is why he placed these people onto the land. But they rejected his claims and abused his messengers. "What shall I do?" he pondered, then decided, "I will send my son, whom I love. Perhaps they will respect him" (Luke 20:13). This is the very scenario the New Testament presents, as stated in the opening words of the Book of Hebrews, "In the past God spoke to our forefathers through the prophets at many times and in various ways, but in these last days he has spoken to us by his Son" (Heb. 1:1–2). Here is a greater messenger, indeed the greatest and last. As Hebrews goes on to exclaim, "How shall we escape if we ignore such a great salvation" as the one he provides and proclaims (Heb. 2:3).

The wicked tenants, however, saw this not as an opportunity to repent but rather to advance their rebellion. Jesus says, "When the tenants saw him, they talked the matter over. 'This is the heir,' they said. 'Let's kill him, and the inheritance will be ours.' So they threw him out of the vineyard and killed him'" (Luke 20:14–15).

This is how the New Testament presents Israel's rejection of Jesus Christ, in these terms he spoke on the eve of his wrongful arrest and murder. God had done all that could be expected and more. He had planted his people with expectation of their fruitfulness. He sent the prophets to warn and to woo them. At the critical juncture he sent his beloved Son, but even him they rejected, abused, and finally killed. As the extent of his grace increased to the full, so too did the extent of their guilt. "What then," Jesus concludes, "will the owner of the vineyard do to them? He will come and kill those tenants and give the vineyard to others" (Luke 20:15–16).

God is patient, but there is an end to his offer of grace, an end that was reached in Israel's rejection of his Son. John 1:11 says, "He came to that which was his own, but his own did not receive him." The result was a terrible judgment and Israel's expulsion from God's vineyard, which in A.D. 70 was revealed in the destruction of their city by the Romans. "Because of their transgression," Paul explains, "salvation has come to the Gentiles" (Rom. 11:11), and now through the gospel all nations are called to repent and believe so as to bear the fruit God desires from his vineyard.

The parable of the wicked tenants tells the story of Israel's rebellion and rejection, but it also points to the fall of humankind as a whole. God is the Creator of the entire human race, whom he made to bear his image and do his will. But humanity has rebelled against God, denied his right to rule, and fought against his will through sin and unbelief. These wicked tenants betray the enmity of every person in rebellion against God. Just as the Jews put God's Son to death, so does the great mass of humankind reject him today, crucifying Jesus all over again through scornful unbelief. Therefore the judgment spoken of here is a judgment that will come to all the world, Jerusalem's fall a mere prelude to the wrath of God against all the rebel earth.

Son and Heir

Luke tells us that Jesus' hearers grasped the meaning of this parable all too well and thus were driven to a rage against him. They realized that Jesus was talking about himself as the son, and this shows his clear understanding of his mission and his coming death.

First, Jesus presents himself in line with the true prophets. Like them, he brought a divine message of God's rights and expectations, calling the people to repentance and belief. This is the answer to the question regarding his authority, which the religious leaders had questioned at the beginning of this chapter. Like the prophets, Jesus spoke from and for God. But the parable goes further and presents Jesus in his unique identity, not merely as a servant like the prophets but as God's beloved Son.

All through church history there have been those who denied Jesus' full divinity. Over the last several generations, some scholars have tried to maintain that Jesus never identified himself as God's unique Son, that the doctrine of the Trinity is the invention of church theologians. Yet what do we have here but Jesus Christ speaking of himself as God's beloved Son who came to earth? This is the same truth so famously expressed in John's Gospel: "For God so loved the world that he gave his one and only Son, that whoever believes in him shall not perish but have eternal life" (John 3:16).

The parable shows not only Jesus' understanding of himself but also of the events about to take place. Alexander Maclaren comments on the marvel of Jesus' composure as he spoke of his cross:

> Nothing is more remarkable in the parable than the calmness of Jesus in announcing His impending fate. He knows it all, and His voice has no tremor, as He tells it as though He were speaking of another. . . . He is ready for the Cross, and its nearness has no terror, not because He was impassive, or free from the shrinking proper to flesh, but because He was resolved to save. Therefore He was resolved to suffer.[2]

Jesus came to Israel with a genuine call to salvation, a genuine offer for them to repent and return to God in faith. Nonetheless, from the beginning he had seen the cross at the end of his journey. As early as Luke 9, he said to his disciples, "Listen carefully to what I am about to tell you: The Son of Man is going to be betrayed into the hands of men" (Luke 9:44–45). Here at the end of his journey, his view has not changed in the least. David Wenham writes, "The parable makes it clear that Jesus sees his own death as the climax of the people's rejection of God's invitation to them to fulfill their proper role, an invitation brought first by the prophets and then by Jesus. But their rejection of the 'son' . . . is an unparalleled and unprecedented act of rebellion against the 'father'."[3] By rejecting Jesus, Israel failed its greatest test and cast away its final chance. That is Jesus' description of what was about to happen, a prophecy that would soon be fulfilled in his death and then in God's judgment on faithless Israel.

Furthermore, Jesus explains why this would happen, exposing the motives of those who even then were plotting his murder. For all their pious words they hated Jesus because they hated God. Rather than serving God and gladly offering him the fruit of his vineyard, their whole hypocritical religion of works and outward show was for their benefit and glory. It was out of hostility to God that they rejected Jesus, just as people reject him today in order to continue living for themselves and not for God. Jesus' coming presented Israel with an opportunity for salvation, through repentance and faith in him. The proclamation of his gospel presents us with the same, with the same warning of judgment for all who reject the Son and therefore the Father who sent him.

The Rejected Stone

And yet, that is not what you would conclude from the people's immediate reaction to Jesus' parable. "May this never be!" they cried, surely concerned more about their loss of privilege than the injustice toward God's Son (Luke 20:16). Jesus' reply cut short their objection, quoting from Psalm 118, an Old Testament passage that speaks about the Messiah and confirms what Jesus had just declared. "What is the meaning of that which is written," he asked, "The stone the builders rejected has become the capstone?" (Luke 20:17). According to the Scriptures, Jesus thus proved, the Messiah would be rejected by the people, just as it would unfold in the days to come.

There is a tradition dating from the building of Solomon's temple that relates to this theme. The great stones were quarried and shaped at a distant site, according to the careful instructions of the architects, then hauled up to the temple site where they could be assembled without the noise of stonecutting. Early in the project a stone was sent up that did not seem to fit anywhere, so the builders cast it aside and forgot all about it. Later, when the temple was nearly complete, they sent word to the quarry that they were ready to receive the capstone, the one stone specially fitted to go in last and hold the others in place. The word came back that such a stone had been sent up long before, and only after a long search did the builders realize their mistake. Finding the cast-off capstone, they discovered that it fit perfectly. The stone the builders rejected had become the capstone, just as the rejected Jesus Christ would become the one on whom our salvation depends.[4]

According to the New International Version (NIV), Jesus is described here as the capstone, the one stone that holds together God's living temple. However, the word is better rendered as "the cornerstone." A cornerstone performs two key functions. It anchors the whole construction and also establishes the lines along which it is to be built. When you were going to start a major construction project, the first thing you did was lay the cornerstone, often with great ceremony. In the same way, Jesus is the cornerstone for our salvation.

I can think of at least three ways in which Jesus is the cornerstone for Christians. First, he is the cornerstone on which our knowledge of God is built, for it is in his face, Paul writes, that we see "the light of the knowledge of the glory of God" (2 Cor. 4:6). "Anyone who has seen me has seen the Father," Jesus declared (John 14:9). Hebrews 1:3

says, "The Son is the radiance of God's glory and the exact representation of his being." Similarly, Jesus is the cornerstone for the building of the church, which rests upon the sufficiency of his saving death and resurrection, and arises from the proclamation of his gospel. So also he is the cornerstone for the erection of every true spiritual life. We are saved to be "conformed to the likeness of [God's] Son, that he might be the firstborn among many brothers" (Rom. 8:29). Therefore if we want to know God, if we want to grow as God's people, if we want to have eternal life, all of these must rest upon and build upon Jesus Christ and his work. Thus Peter wrote, quoting the prophet Isaiah, "See, I lay a stone in Zion, a chosen and precious cornerstone; and the one who trusts in him will never be put to shame" (1 Peter 2:6).

"The stone the builders rejected has become the cornerstone," Jesus reminded them. These words not only speak of his rejection and death but also reminded his disciples to anticipate his resurrection. He would be despised and rejected, yes, and even put to death by wicked men—yet still he would become the cornerstone. How is that? Peter explained it at Pentecost, several weeks later, "You, with the help of wicked men, put him to death by nailing him to the cross. But God raised him from the dead, freeing him from the agony of death, because it was impossible for death to keep its hold on him" (Acts 2:23–24). Here God's agenda confronts the plans of people, for what humanity has rejected God has established as the cornerstone of his church.

Jesus' parables as a whole call his hearers to take a stand on the issues, to make a decision, to choose a position. So it is here. If it is true that Jesus Christ, though rejected of men, is established by God as the Savior of the world and cornerstone of God's true temple, then the great matter of life and death is how you stand in relation to him. According to the Bible, Jesus Christ is placed by God as a stone before the world, and our destiny is determined by our attitude toward him. Yes, he is the Savior for all who trust in him. But, Jesus added, "Everyone who falls on that stone will be broken to pieces, but he on whom it falls will be crushed" (Luke 20:18).

In 1 Corinthians 1:23 the apostle Paul says that Christ crucified was a stumbling block to the Jews, for the idea of a humble Savior was an offense to their religious pride. But it is not merely the Jews that Jesus challenges, for Paul adds that Christ is foolishness to the Gentiles. His gospel is a way of salvation that offends the wisdom of the world. All this is still true today, that Christ's gospel offends the world's pride and wisdom. The cross proclaims people's need of a Savior; his blood speaks forth of our sin. Why else was God's Son nailed to a cross to suffer and die? Not to inspire a vague sentiment of adoration in us, but as Paul says in Ephesians 1:7, so that we may "have redemption through his blood, the forgiveness of sins." The angel told Joseph, "You are to name him Jesus, because he will save his people from their sins" (Matt. 1:21). His death tells of the punishment we have deserved, his resurrection of a salvation that is by grace alone and to God's glory alone. Still today, this scheme of salvation—God's Son coming into this world to die for our sins, that we might be forgiven through his blood and inwardly renewed by his resurrection life—is an offense to people. It challenges their belief about themselves and how they want to come to God. Jesus is a stumbling block to everyone who will not humble himself or herself in repentance and faith.

That is not all, for, Jesus says, "He on whom it falls will be crushed" (Luke 20:18). That was true for Jerusalem.

Having rejected God's Son, the Jews fell to the sword a generation later. Even that was but a prelude to the final judgment that is still to come. Christ's future return in glory will mean destruction to his enemies, the coming of his kingdom a stone that crushes those who oppose him in this world (see Dan. 2:44).

God Sent His Son

This chapter concludes our studies in Jesus' parables. It does so fittingly, proclaiming, as do the parables as a whole, the utter necessity of commitment to Christ and the priorities of his kingdom. Just as when Jesus first told these parables, they now put us on the spot. They test us and demand a decision we cannot avoid. Will we turn to him? Will we give God what is due to him, seeing that he has sent his Son? Will we allow Jesus to reshape our lives, to upend our world? Ultimately it is our eternal destiny that is at stake.

The parables challenge us by showing us what we really are like. For these stories are not only about some other or hypothetical people—they are about us. We can summarize what they show in three terms. First, the parables expose our wickedness. The parable of the good Samaritan showed our lack of love for those in need; the barren fig tree depicted our spiritual fruitlessness; the rich fool showed our greed, while the shrewd manager challenged our lazy indifference to the things of God. Add these up, and you have various components of our wickedness in sin.

Similarly, the parables expose us in our folly. We are like the figures in these parables, unwilling to humbly ask of God, clinging to our self-righteousness, seeking security in things that will perish.

Finally, the parables depict our alienation from God

and our ignorance of him. Isn't that why we find it hard to pray, though God is so good and free in his giving? Isn't that why we, like the Pharisees, settle for religious externals? Isn't that why we, like these wicked tenants, resent God's claims and demands, striving so violently against his rule?

Jesus wants us to see and accept these things because they are true about our condition. This is the problem: we are wicked and foolish and alienated from God. Accepting the reality and magnitude of this problem prepares us to receive the answer Jesus came to bring, indeed, to accept Jesus as the Answer God has sent. Luke 20:13 expresses the great gospel truth that makes all the difference to those who believe. God said, "I will send my son, whom I love." This is God's answer to the problem of humanity—to our problem as individuals—as revealed in the parables: "God sent his Son." What wonderful good news this is—news that changes everything, that turns our world upside down. Here is the good news that calls us to come to God in faith, worshiping him with our lives, submitting gladly to his rule: God sent his Son!

Humankind is wicked and under God's just wrath; the parables have made that plain. Here is the answer: "God sent his Son." Into the vineyard came Jesus Christ to be crucified, bearing the sins of all who look to him in faith. For all who repent and believe, he has become our righteousness, the forgiveness of our sins. The parables declare the folly of humanity, but here is the answer: "God sent his Son." For all who enter into union with him, the Bible says, "He has become for us wisdom from God" (1 Cor. 1:30). The risen Jesus sends God's Spirit to renew our minds as he instructs us through God's Word, challenging us as he has done in the study of these parables.

Finally, the parables reveal that through sin and folly, we are separated from God, alienated from his light and life, "without hope," as Paul puts it, "and without God in the world" (Eph. 2:12). But here is the answer: God sent his Son. "When we were still powerless," Paul explains, "Christ died for the ungodly. . . . God demonstrates his own love for us in this: While we were still sinners, Christ died for us" (Rom. 5:6–8). God sent his Son! Paul adds, "God was reconciling the world to himself in Christ, not counting men's sins against them" (2 Cor. 5:19). "Now in Christ Jesus you who once were far away have been brought near through the blood of Christ" (Eph. 2:13). We were alienated, enemies of God, but he sent his Son and now "he is our peace" (Eph. 2:14), having reconciled us to God through the cross.

God sent his Son! Here is the stone upon which many stumble and are crushed. But if we repent and believe, if we submit our lives to Jesus to have him turn them upside down, inside out, to reorder them according to his priorities, his truth, and his love, then this stone the builders rejected will be the cornerstone for a whole new life, one that is led by Christ and blessed by God. "The stone the builders rejected has become the capstone," says the psalm. But then it adds, as we must surely agree, "The Lord has done this, and it is marvelous in our eyes" (Ps. 118:22–23).

Is it difficult? Certainly, for Jesus demands no less than a revolution in the manner of our life, starting with a new ruler enthroned within our hearts and extending to the new administration of all his saving realm. But what a difference it makes that the One who demands such sacrifice and change held back nothing in his love for us. This parable of the tenants, demanding surrender to the claims of the sovereign God, was spoken by Jesus just days before he surrendered his will to the anguish of the cross, that we might have life. And it is from the shadow of that cross that he says to us even today, "If anyone would come after me, he must deny himself and take up his cross daily and follow me. For whoever wants to save his life will lose it, but whoever loses his life for me will save it" (Luke 9:23–24).

Notes

Chapter 1: A Farmer Sowing Seed

1 Harry A. Ironside, *Addresses on the Gospel of Luke* (Neptune, N.J.: Loizeaux Brothers, 1947), 239.

2 J. C. Ryle, *Expository Thoughts on Luke*, 2 vols. (Carlisle, Pa.: Banner of Truth, 1986), 2:250–51.

3 James Montgomery Boice, *Matthew*, 2 vols. (Grand Rapids, Mich.: Baker, 2001), 1:233–34.

Chapter 2: The Good Samaritan

1 Darrell A. Bock, *Luke*, 2 vols. (Grand Rapids, Mich.: Baker, 1996), 2:1031.

2 Kenneth E. Bailey, *Through Peasant Eyes* (Grand Rapids, Mich.: Eerdmans, 1980), 50.

3 J. C. Ryle, *Expository Thoughts on Luke*, 2 vols. (Carlisle, Pa.: Banner of Truth, 1986), 1:270.

4 See Bailey, *Through Peasant Eyes*, 39.

5 Charles Haddon Spurgeon, *The Parables and Miracles of Our Lord*, 3 vols. (Grand Rapids, Mich.: Baker, 1993), 3:210.

Chapter 3: A Parable on Prayer

1 D. Martyn Lloyd-Jones, *God's Ultimate Purpose: An Exposition of Ephesians 1* (Grand Rapids, Mich.: Baker, 1978), 326.
2 Arland Hultgren, *Commentary on the Parables of Jesus* (Grand Rapids, Mich.: Eerdmans, 2000), 229.
3 A. W. Tozer, *The Knowledge of the Holy* (New York: HarperCollins, 1961), 127–28.
4 J. I. Packer, *Knowing God* (Downers Grove, Ill.: InterVarsity Press, 1979), 182.
5 Philip Graham Ryken, *When You Pray* (Wheaton, Ill.: Crossway, 2000), 56.
6 William Hendriksen, *Luke* (Grand Rapids, Mich.: Baker, 1978), 612.
7 Ibid.
8 Arthur W. Pink, *The Sovereignty of God* (Grand Rapids, Mich.: Baker, 1975), 174.
9 J. C. Ryle, *Expository Thoughts on Luke*, 2 vols. (Carlisle, Pa.: Banner of Truth, 1986), 2:12.

Chapter 4: The Rich Fool

1 Alexander Maclaren, *Expositions of Holy Scripture*, 17 vols. (Grand Rapids, Mich.: Baker, 1982), 9:339, 340.
2 John Grisham, *The Testament* (New York: Doubleday, 1999), 285.
3 J. C. Ryle, *Expository Thoughts on Luke*, 2 vols. (Carlisle, Pa.: Banner of Truth, 1986), 2:76.
4 Maclaren, *Expositions of Holy Scripture*, 339.
5 Leon Morris, *Luke* (Grand Rapids, Mich.: Eerdmans, 1974), 213.
6 Ryle, *Expository Thoughts on Luke*, 74.
7 William M. Taylor, *The Parables of Our Savior Expounded and Illustrated* (New York: A. C. Armstrong and Son, 1900), 274–75.
8 Jeremiah Burroughs, *The Rare Jewel of Christian Contentment* (Carlisle, Pa.: Banner of Truth, 1964), 45.
9 R. Kent Hughes, *Luke*, 2 vols. (Wheaton, Ill.: Crossway, 1998), 2:50.

Chapter 5: The Barren Fig Tree

1 John Piper, *Seeing and Savoring Jesus Christ* (Wheaton, Ill.: Crossway, 2001), 103.

2 John Calvin, A *Harmony of the Gospels*, 3 vols. (Grand Rapids, Mich.: Eerdmans, 1972), 2:95.
3 William Arnot, *Parables of Our Lord* (Grand Rapids, Mich.: Kregel, 1981), 379.
4 J. C. Ryle, *Expository Thoughts on Luke*, 2 vols. (Carlisle, Pa.: Banner of Truth, 1986), 2:114–15.
5 F. F. Bruce, *The Epistle to the Hebrews* (Grand Rapids, Mich.: Eerdmans, 1990), 79–80.
6 Arnot, *Parables of Our Lord*, 385–86.

Chapter 6: The Mustard Seed and Yeast

1 J. C. Ryle, *Expository Thoughts on Luke*, 2 vols. (Carlisle, Pa.: Banner of Truth, 1986), 2:125–26.
2 See John Legg, *The Footsteps of God* (Hertfordshire, U.K.: Evangelical Press, 1986), 295.
3 Arland Hultgren, *Commentary on the Parables of Jesus* (Grand Rapids, Mich.: Eerdmans, 2000), 406.
4 James Montgomery Boice, *Whatever Happened to the Gospel of Grace?* (Wheaton, Ill.: Crossway, 2001), 83–84.
5 Marcellus Kik, *Church and State: The Story of Two Kingdoms* (New York: Thomas Nelson, 1963), 85.
6 Hugh Martin, *Christ for Us: Sermons of Hugh Martin* (Carlisle, Pa.: Banner of Truth, 1998), 237.

Chapter 7: The Great Banquet

1 J. C. Ryle, *Expository Thoughts on Luke*, 2 vols. (Carlisle, Pa.: Banner of Truth, 1986), 2:160.
2 Thomas Wolfe; see Ravi Zacharias, *Can Man Live Without God?* (Dallas: Word, 1994), 69–70.
3 Marcus Dods, *The Parables of Our Lord* (London: Hodder and Stoughton, n.d.), 95–96.
4 James Montgomery Boice, *Matthew*, 2 vols. (Grand Rapids, Mich.: Baker, 2001), 1:468.
5 Ryle, *Expository Thoughts on Luke*, 165.
6 See Boice, *Matthew*, 1:469–70.

Chapter 8: Three Lost Treasures

1 Marcus Dods, *The Parables of Our Lord* (London: Hodder and Stoughton, n.d.), 107.

2 Joachim Jeremias, *Theology of the New Testament* (New York: Scribner, 1971), 115–16.

3 Kenneth E. Bailey, *Poet and Peasant* (Grand Rapids, Mich.: Eerdmans, 1976), 164.

4 D. Martyn Lloyd-Jones, *The Cross* (Wheaton, Ill.: Crossway, 1986), 157–58.

5 Aldous Huxley, *Ends and Means* (London: Chatto & Windus, 1946), 273, 270.

6 A. W. Tozer, *The Knowledge of the Holy* (San Francisco: HarperCollins, 1961), 98.

7 Charles Haddon Spurgeon, *Miracles and Parables of Our Lord*, 3 vols. (Grand Rapids, Mich.: Baker, 1993), 3:381–92.

8 Alexander Maclaren, *Expositions of Holy Scripture*, 17 vols. (Grand Rapids, Mich.: Baker, 1982), 9b:70.

Chapter 9: The Shrewd Manager

1 R. Kent Hughes, *Luke*, 2 vols. (Wheaton, Ill.: Crossway, 1998), 2:147.

2 Leon Morris, *Luke* (Downers Grove, Ill.: InterVarsity Press, 1974), 246.

3 Kenneth E. Bailey, *Poet and Peasant* (Grand Rapids, Mich.: Eerdmans, 1976), 97–110.

4 Alexander Maclaren, *Expositions of Holy Scripture*, 17 vols. (Grand Rapids, Mich.: Baker, 1982), 9b:76.

5 Ibid., 9b:77.

6 William Hendriksen, *Luke* (Grand Rapids, Mich.: Baker, 1978), 770.

7 John Calvin, *A Harmony of the Gospels*, 3 vols. (Grand Rapids, Mich.: Eerdmans, 1972), 2:112.

8 David Wenham, *The Parables of Jesus* (Downers Grove, Ill.: InterVarsity Press, 1989), 166.

9 See Hughes, *Luke*, 2:151.

Chapter 10: The Rich Man and the Beggar

1 William Hendriksen, *Luke* (Grand Rapids, Mich.: Baker, 1978), 782.
2 J. C. Ryle, *Expository Thoughts on Luke*, 2 vols. (Carlisle, Pa.: Banner of Truth, 1986), 2:212.
3 John Calvin, *A Harmony of the Gospels* (Grand Rapids, Mich.: Eerdmans, 1972), 119.
4 James Montgomery Boice, *The Parables of Jesus* (Chicago: Moody Press, 1983), 214.
5 Charles Haddon Spurgeon, *Miracles and Parables of Our Lord* (Grand Rapids, Mich.: Baker, 1993), 421–22.
6 A. W. Tozer, *The Tozer Pulpit*, book 1, *Selections from His Pulpit Ministry* (Camp Hill, Pa.: Christian Publications, 1994), 89.
7 William Arnot, *Parables of Our Lord* (Grand Rapids, Mich.: Kregel, 1981), 481.
8 Ryle, *Expository Thoughts on Luke*, 215–16.

Chapter 11: The Pharisee and the Tax Collector

1 Jonathan Edwards, *Jonathan Edwards on Revival* (Carlisle, Pa.: Banner of Truth, 1965), 137.
2 Augustine, *City of God*, (New York: Doubleday, 1958), 310.
3 C. S. Lewis, *Mere Christianity* (New York: Macmillan, 1958), 111.
4 Darrell A. Bock, *Luke*, 2 vols. (Grand Rapids, Mich.: Baker, 1996), 2:1461.
5 John Calvin, *Institutes of the Christian Religion*, ed. John T. McNeill, 2 vols. (Philadelphia: Westminster Press, 1960), 1:726.
6 Thomas Watson: *A Body of Divinity* (Carlisle, Pa.: Banner of Truth, 1958), 226.
7 J. I. Packer: "Introductory Essay," in James Buchanon, *The Doctrine of Justification: An Outline of Its History in the Church and of Its Exposition from Scripture* (London: Banner of Truth, 1961), vii.
8 Kenneth E. Bailey, *Through Peasant Eyes* (Grand Rapids, Mich.: Eerdmans, 1980), 154.

Chapter 12: The Returning King

1 Norval Geldenhuys, *The Gospel of Luke* (Grand Rapids, Mich.: Eerdmans, 1951), 474.

2 Charles Haddon Spurgeon, *Parables and Miracles of Our Lord*, 3 vols. (Grand Rapids, Mich.: Baker, 1993), 3:488.
3 Joachim Jeremias, *The Parables of Jesus* (Saddle River, N.J.: Prentice Hall, 1972), 49.
4 Matthew Henry, *Commentary on the Whole Bible*, 6 vols. (Peabody, Mass.: Hendrickson, n.d.), 5:635.

Chapter 13: The Wicked Tenants

1 Charles Haddon Spurgeon, *The Metropolitan Tabernacle Pulpit*, 63 vols. (Pasadena, Tex.: Pilgrim, 1975), 33:137.
2 Alexander Maclaren, *Expositions of Holy Scripture*, 17 vols. (Grand Rapids, Mich.: Baker, 1982), 9:193.
3 David Wenham, *The Parables of Jesus* (Downers Grove, Ill.: Inter-Varsity Press, 1989), 127.
4 See James Montgomery Boice, *Romans*, 4 vols. (Grand Rapids, Mich.: Baker, 1993), 3:1146–47.

Discussion Questions

Chapter 1: A Farmer Sowing Seed

1. What is a parable? What is it about parables that makes them so effective at confronting us with truth? How is it that, as the author states, we not only interpret parables but parables interpret us?
2. According to this passage, why did Jesus teach in parables? Was it fair for him to use the parables to reveal to some and conceal to others? Discuss.
3. Jesus said that the kingdom of God is like "a farmer sowing seed." What does this tell us about how the Lord's work is done in this world? What does it tell us about the place of God's Word in Christian ministry? How does this, as the author asserts, provide a philosophy of history?
4. What are the three soils of unbelief as Jesus explains them? How do you see these keeping people you know from trusting and following Christ?

5. How do the three bad soils speak to worldliness or unbelief working within your own heart? What priorities do these soils point to for your prayer life and spiritual growth?
6. How can we tell that our hearts are like the good soil Jesus described? How can our hearts become more like this good soil?
7. What does it mean for Christians to bear fruit? Why is it so important?
8. Pray for God's regenerating work in the hearts of non-Christians you know. Pray for God's work in you, to turn up the hardened soil and make good soil out of your heart.

Chapter 2: The Good Samaritan

1. How would most people answer the question, "What must I do to inherit eternal life?"
2. The lawyer in this parable sought to justify himself by his works. But what was his actual attitude toward the requirements of God's law? How are people like that today?
3. How does the parable depict "hypocrisy and externalism"? What was the problem with the priest and the Levite? How do we follow their bad example today?
4. Work through the actions of the good Samaritan and discuss how they are a model of Christian ministry and compassion.
5. What is the answer to the question, "Who is my neighbor?" What are the implications for your own life?
6. What is the doctrine of justification? Why is this the most important topic in this passage?
7. The author states that whenever someone comes to Jesus seeking to be justified by his works, Jesus directs him to the law. Why? And why can't our works justify us?

8. The law says, "Do this and live." But Jesus says, "Live, now do this." What is the difference between the two? What are the implications for our lives?

Chapter 3: A Parable on Prayer

1. What does it take for God to answer our prayers? What do you think makes prayer "work"?
2. How does the parable of "the friend at midnight" give us confidence that God answers our prayers? How does this teaching encourage our prayer lives?
3. Does prayer make a difference? Does prayer change things? If it does, how does that relate to the idea of God's sovereignty?
4. In verses 11–13, Jesus compares our heavenly Father to human fathers. What do you think about the idea that God is our Father? What does the passage say about it? How does this encourage us in prayer?
5. Discuss Jesus' statement in verses 9–10. Is this true? What are the implications of these verses?
6. What are we to make of the "problem" of unanswered prayers?
7. Why is the Holy Spirit the best gift God has to give us? In what ways should we pray for the Holy Spirit's work in our lives?
8. How will this parable's teaching make a difference in your prayer life?

Chapter 4: The Rich Fool

1. The apostle Paul warned Timothy against the dangers of money. Can you think of any biblical examples of people who were judged because of their greed? What do these examples tell us?

2. When the man asked for Jesus' help in a financial dispute, why wouldn't Jesus get involved? What lessons can we draw from this?

3. Jesus said that life does not consist in the abundance of possessions. Can you think of blessings that cannot be bought with money? What does this suggest regarding the relationship between happiness and money?

4. The author claims that the rich man was a "practical atheist." What do you see to support this? Why does Paul say in Colossians 3:5 that greed is "idolatry"?

5. Why do people think money will provide them security for the future? In the parable, what effect did the rich man's greed really have on his future? Given Jesus' teaching, how should we seek security?

6. What does it mean to be "rich toward God"? How does Jesus' teaching challenge your priorities?

7. What are some practical implications of this passage regarding our use of money? What habits or attitudes regarding money should you bring to God in prayer? Conclude your discussion by praying for God's help in rearranging your financial priorities and by thanking him for his abundant provision to all who trust in him.

Chapter 5: The Barren Fig Tree

1. What was Jesus' reaction to the tragedies of his day as described in this passage? Why are tragedies a call for sinners to repent? What is repentance?

2. Why do we hear so little today about God's judgment? Why is it so important for believers to recognize and speak about this? How were the tragedies Jesus spoke of similar to God's coming judgment?

3. When people die or suffer in tragedies, does that suggest that God is out to get them? How would you explain this to a non-Christian?
4. How is the fig tree similar to people within the church? How does the call to bear fruit summarize the Christian life?
5. How does this parable speak about Christ's patient ministry to us?
6. Who is speaking in verses 8–9? What is the difference between relying on God's grace and presuming on God's grace?
7. What has God done to promote your spiritual growth? What are you to do in response to his mercy? Discuss ways in which God is prompting you to bear fruit and how you can follow through.

Chapter 6: The Mustard Seed and Yeast

1. Why is it hard for us to believe when things aren't going well? How was this true for Jesus' disciples during his life?
2. How does the history of the church prove that big things come from small beginnings? How does this work in our individual spiritual lives?
3. The author says, "We find it hard to believe that small and weak beginnings can lead to something great." Why is this? How does this parable challenge our attitude? How does it reshape our thoughts about ministry?
4. How does the parable of the yeast speak of the gospel's penetrating power? How have you experienced the gospel working in your life?
5. In what way is God's kingdom "hidden" or "buried" in this present world? Where should we look to find it?
6. Is there anything small God wants you to start? In what ways might God turn that something small into something big?

Chapter 7: The Great Banquet

1. Have you ever attended a great feast? If so, describe what it was like?
2. The author says that salvation life in God's kingdom is a feast. How is that so? What are the food and drink that God serves to his people?
3. Who does God invite to his salvation feast? How do you get an invitation?
4. This parable depicts a number of revealing excuses for not accepting God's invitation. What are they and how do they happen today? Have you ever made these excuses? Do you still make them? What is the implication of rejecting God's offer of salvation?
5. How does this parable inform and motivate our work of evangelism? How might you follow this example and deliver God's invitations to eternal life?
6. Most hosts look down on the poor or unworthy? Why is God different? How does his attitude bring glory to his name?
7. As you study this parable, where do you see yourself fitting into the picture? How is God calling on you to respond?

Chapter 8: Three Lost Treasures

1. Have you ever lost something of great value to you? How did you feel while you were looking for it? What was it like when you found it?
2. Why were the Pharisees offended that Jesus ate with "tax collectors and sinners"? Do you have or have you ever had that attitude toward others? What is wrong with it?
3. What are the three different ways people become lost, as depicted in these parables? What dangers do they suggest that Christians need to avoid?

4. How does the prodigal son's unloving attitude toward his father depict sinful humanity's attitude in rebellion to God? The author points this out as the heart of human sin before God. Do you agree? How does the prodigal's experience typify our experience in sin?
5. The author describes the parable of the prodigal son as "a vivid depiction of the sinner's repentance." What steps of repentance does he take? How does this parable encourage us to begin the difficult path of repentance?
6. What does the parable of the prodigal son teach us about God's love for sinners? Consider the particular details in the father's response. What do they say about God's love?
7. Reflect upon the reaction of the elder brother. What dangers does his behavior warn us against? Discuss.

Chapter 9: The Shrewd Manager

1. If you were to look at someone's checkbook, how much do you think it would tell you about his or her values? What does your checkbook say about you?
2. Consider the behavior of the shrewd manager. What is there to commend in him? What might we criticize?
3. Jesus commented, "The children of this age are more shrewd in dealing with their own generation than are the children of the light." What did he mean? Who are the children of this age? How do they contrast with children of the light?
4. Is it possible that worldly people show more resourcefulness in worldly things than Christians do in spiritual things? Discuss.
5. How does this parable speak to our need to be prepared to stand before God and give an account of our lives?
6. Jesus goes on to teach about the need for godly stewardship of our wealth. What are the points that he makes? Does anything he says have special relevance for you?

7. Why is our stewardship of little things so important? What experience have you had with this principle? Are there little things in which God is asking you to be faithful?

Chapter 10: The Rich Man and the Beggar

1. Why do you think money comes up so often in Jesus' parables? What is it about money that is so closely linked with spiritual things?
2. Discuss the rich man in this parable. What was his attitude toward possessions? Toward people?
3. Jesus says that no one can serve two masters. How does this work out in our lives today? What challenge does it lay before us? What are the stakes involved?
4. Contrast the difference between the rich man's and Lazarus's funeral. Contrast their different receptions in the afterlife. What is the lesson here?
5. What does this parable indicate to us about the life after death? Does this portrayal encourage us to believe there will be second chances to believe and be saved after we die?
6. Do you believe in the reality of hell as a place of torment? If so, why? If not, why not? What does this parable have to say about the subject? What other passages does the author refer to in order to present the biblical view?
7. Why won't people believe even if they received a visitor from the dead? What, then, must people do to believe and be saved? What does this parable indicate about our approach to evangelism?

Chapter 11: The Pharisee and the Tax Collector

1. If a tax collector was the ultimate scum of ancient Judaism, what kind of person fits that description today? How can

someone like that ever become right with God? Can you think of any examples like this?

2. Consider the Pharisee's prayer. What was wrong with it?
3. C. S. Lewis said, "The essential vice, the utmost evil, is Pride." Do you agree with that? Do you disagree? What is it about pride that makes it so evil and harmful to our souls?
4. Now consider the tax collector's prayer. Contrast the two ways of coming to God as shown by the two men in this parable. Is one way just as good as another?
5. The author says, "Humility is absolutely necessary to salvation." Is that true? If so, why?
6. This parable is considered a classic illustration of the doctrine of justification. What does it teach about justification? What does the doctrine mean and why is it important for us to get it right?
7. What is the mercy seat? How does it figure into this parable? Why is it noteworthy to us today?
8. The author concludes with Paul's personal testimony as given in Philippians 3. How does your testimony relate to the teaching of this parable? What kind of math are you using in your spiritual balance sheet?

Chapter 12: The Returning King

1. When in his ministry did Jesus teach this parable? How did his circumstances prompt the teaching he gave here?
2. What does this parable have to say about "a Christian view of history"? According to Jesus, what is really going on in this world?
3. What is a mina? What does it signify in this parable? What are we to do with the "mina" Jesus gives to us?

4. What do the returning king's rewards teach us about Christ's distribution of rewards to his loyal servants? Why does this show his grace in abundance?

5. Will there be rewards in heaven? What kind of rewards, if any, do you think they will be? Does this violate the idea of salvation by grace alone? Should we be motivated now by the idea of future rewards?

6. One servant was condemned. What was his real problem? What does this parable teach us about God's judgment in the return of Christ?

7. How does this parable challenge you to live more boldly and faithfully for Jesus? Pray in light of what you have learned.

Chapter 13: The Wicked Tenants

1. Have you ever been a tenant? What was your relationship like with your landlord? Were you a good tenant?

2. Why were the Pharisees so hostile to Jesus? What lesson is there in this for us?

3. What or who does the vineyard in this parable represent? What does it say about them?

4. How does this parable tell of Israel's record of sin? And how does it tell the story of God's gracious attitude toward his people?

5. In the parable the owner of the vineyard is faced with a difficult problem. What is it? What was his solution to this problem? To what does this really refer?

6. How does this parable confirm that Jesus considered himself to be God's Son and the Savior God sent into the world? What does he expect his listeners to do in response to this revelation?

7. What does it mean that Jesus is "the stone the builders rejected" and "the capstone of the building?"
8. How does this parable sum up the whole of Jesus' teaching in the parables? According to this vital teaching, what should our response be to this and all the other parables? Discuss and pray.

Index of Scripture

Index of Subjects and Names

Richard D. Phillips (B.A., University of Michigan; M.B.A., University of Pennsylvania; M.Div., Westminster Theological Seminary) is senior minister of First Presbyterian Church in Coral Springs/Margate, Florida. He is also speaker-at-large for the Alliance of Confessing Evangelicals and director of the Philadelphia Conference on Reformation Theology.

An officer in the United States Army for thirteen years, Phillips commanded various tank and armored cavalry units and served as assistant professor of leadership at the United States Military Academy, West Point, before resigning with the rank of major.

He is the author of *Mighty to Save: Discovering God's Grace in the Miracles of Jesus*, *Encounters with Jesus: When Ordinary People Met the Savior*, and *Faith Victorious: Finding Strength and Hope from Hebrews 11*. He lives in South Florida with his wife, Sharon, and their four children, Hannah, Matthew, Jonathan, and Helen.